Invest Like
the Successful Pros

Robert E. Johnson

University of New Haven Press
West Haven, Connecticut

Library of Congress Cataloging in Publication Data

Robert E. Johnson, Invest Like the Successful Pros, Investment
problems, Selecting your investment assets, Monitor and adjust
investments, Bibliography, Index

ISBN 0-936285-20-6

Library of Congress Catalog Card Number: 92-083940

Printed in the United States of America

Dedicated to:

Barbara
Jackie
&
Tracy

With a special thanks to those who, each in their unique way, contributed to the body of knowledge which made this book possible, including but not limited to:

Stan Abel, Ed Barksdale, Tom Clarke, Paul Daoust, Charlie Ellis, Ed Fiedler, Bill Fouse, Harold Griffin, Peter Lamaison, Ed Leary, Dean LeBaron, M.L. McLaughlin, Peter Neville, Steve Rogers, Charles Schwab, Ted Wallis, & Vaughn West.

CONTENTS

INTRODUCTION

The idea for this book came after years of frustration resulting from exposure to the world of investing. This frustration comes from observing individual or amateur investors, as well as dealing with the professionals who either manage the bulk of the country's securities or sell investment products.

Individuals, in general, seem to give the investment of their savings about as much attention as they do the purchase and maintenance of their automobiles. For most, it's an occasional exiting event but soon becomes ignored and only receives attention when absolutely necessary, such as in an emergency or when they realize they own an expensive "clunker" which they can't do much about except get rid of at a loss. Based upon my experience, most individuals seem to be either overly conservative or overly reckless with their investments. In either case, the investment results have typically been poor.

Those who sell investment products are, more often than not, good sales people with limited knowledge of investments and with a principal, and sometimes only objective of getting commissions from the products they sell. They usually fall into the classification of either brokers or financial planners. They tend to view and discuss an investment strategy in terms of single investment ideas appropriate for a small percent of a person's or fund's investment portfolio rather than how they fit into a broad investment structure or strategy.

And what about those who hire these salespeople - the brokerage firms and other sponsors of products to be sold?

They also seem to be mainly devoted to selling individual investment products and much less concerned as to whether the products are really sound investments, or fit the needs of the buyers, or most important, whether those they've hired to do the selling are really qualified to manage people's life savings. If you've ever looked into the requirements to sell investment products, you know what I mean. Virtually no investment knowledge is required to get employed and only limited knowledge of investments is required before salespeople are turned loose on the public.

The professional money managers who manage the billions of dollars in United States retirement and endowment funds also are part of the frustration which lead to the writing of this book. They are incredibly intelligent, hard working people, many of whom devote their lives to investing. But, as we will discuss later on, most are not able to generate investment returns for their clients which are even equal to the average of the universe in which they invest. That is, if they are stock market investors, most are unable to provide investment returns equal to stock market averages such as the Standard & Poors 500. But despite the evidence which confirms this failure, they charge exorbitant fees and continue to promise clients that they truly have the secret to "beating the market".

I have long been a part of the final group which has contributed to my frustrations. This group is the fund sponsors and trustees as well as the corporate managers who hire and fire the money managers who achieve the generally substandard investment results. My major problem with this group is that they usually manage the investment process on a quarter to quarter basis rather than as a process which can only be truly evaluated over a long period of time. As business managers fall more and more into the mode of managing their businesses for the short term "Wall Street" benefit, so do they tend to view their pension or endowment fund assets the same way.

So what is the purpose of this book? Simply to point out the ways in which the successful professionals manage the investment process and particularly to show that it is just as easy for individuals to successfully manage their investments the same way. Let me give just one example of why I think this is an important issue.

For more than a decade, I had investment responsibility for the pension assets of a large corporation. Of course the assets really belonged to the employees, and the corporation was simply the pension plan sponsor, fiduciary, and administrator. These assets had considerable time and attention devoted to them, as they should have, by management, the board of directors, and external investment "experts".

Retiring employees had the option of taking their pensions in a single "lump sum" distribution as opposed to taking a monthly annuity. Most took this lump sum option because it was the most financially sound option.

So what did we, the pension sponsors, in effect do? We took pieces of a professionally managed pension fund and handed them over to their rightful owners, who frequently had little or no investment knowledge or ability. Many individuals received distributions in excess of $100,000 but, whatever the amount, it was usually more money than they had ever had access to in their lives.

And what did the individuals do with the money? Frequently they either gave it poor self investment management or gave it to a poorly qualified broker or financial planner. I can only assume that there are many horrible stories of people who have "blown" pensions which were built up over many years and which were intended to take care of them in their old age. And worst of all, for people in this stage of life, it's too late to start building assets all over again.

I hope this book will help many individuals avoid future investment disasters.

Robert E. Johnson

CHAPTER 1

Investment Problems
and Issues

CHAPTER I

INVESTMENT PROBLEMS AND ISSUES

THE PROBLEMS

It is often said that the best signal of the stock market peaking is when individuals begin investing in it in full force. While this may be a slight exaggeration, there is none-the-less an element of truth to it . And it is probably as true for other investment markets such as gold and real estate as it is for the stock market.

Why does this happen? Probably because the individual investor reaches a point of being unable to resist the euphoria of "hot" markets as they hit the media headlines each day. If people hear enough about stock, real estate or gold markets going up and see their own investments in the money markets or in savings accounts earning fixed, probably single digit returns, the temptation to participate is more than many can resist. This frequently is the worst time to invest and the unfortunate result is that most individual investors underperform professionals in achieving investment return.

But beyond the emotional factors, my belief is that most professionals outperform individuals because they have a disciplined approach to investing and don't let emotions and neglect override these disciplines. It is not because they have inside information or because they spend their working lives totally immersed in the investment process. Although working full time in the process certainly provides an advantage over most people who invest as a hobby or avocation.

Of course, it is unfair to suggest that all individual investors generate poor returns. Many have had incredibly impressive investment results. But my guess is that most have not and that most pay much less attention to their investible assets than they should. And the frequent reaction to subsequent poor results is to either take a "you can't beat the market" attitude and stay away from it or to allow a poor investment portfolio to drift along unattended.

The individual was not a heavy participant in the 1980's bull market, probably because of being on the losing end of the 1968-70, 1973-74, and 1980-82 significant bear markets. In fact, the individual had over 40% of his investments in equities in the late 1960's and has steadily reduced the allocation to about 20% at the end of the 1980's *. No question, the individual has "dropped out" of the stock market. Strange when, as we will discuss, equities historically have been the highest returning investment choice.

The interesting contrast is that a common practice of professional investors is to use market downturns as the springboard for periods of excellent returns.

Before we get into why professional investors are more successful than individuals, let me give you my definition of the term "professional investor". First of all, it includes those who manage funds belonging to institutions, individuals, or business entities. These funds generally are in the form of pension or endowment funds or public mutual funds. This group of professionals is generally referred to as professional investors.

The second group, in my definition, is those who direct the placement of pools of funds with investment managers and

* Goldman Sachs, EQUITIES SUPPLY & DEMAND, October 1990

who are responsible for the investment results. This group mainly consists of those with responsibility for pension or endowment funds or perhaps large pools of private money. These professionals are frequently referred to as investment fund sponsors.

My definition of a professional investor has one additional and very important ingredient, which is the requirement for an independently verified record of investment performance. This record is as important as the independently kept score of a professional baseball or basketball game, as opposed to relying on the teams to keep their own scores. It is as important as the independently determined winner of a beauty contest, as opposed to leaving the decision to the contestants.

My definition particularly excludes most stock brokers, most investment planners, real estate agents, and others who either do not manage or direct pools of money or do not have an independently verified record of their performance.

Is an independently verified performance record an unreasonable requirement? We're talking about your life savings. Is it any more appropriate to delegate investing to someone with no successful track record than it is to allow someone to operate on you without credentials and a successful background in performing surgery? Would you hire someone to do an important job if they didn't have the education or the experience that the job requires? I doubt it.

Let's now begin to look at some of the ways in which professionals operate and how this process differs from the way individuals manage their money.

REALISTIC EXPECTATIONS

A good starting point is to talk about the kind of returns we should expect from our investments. I believe that most people think that professional investors make much higher returns than they, in fact, do.

Let's look at what the popular investment vehicles did in the 1980's, a period of unusually good returns by historical standards. For the 10 years, United States equities (stocks) returned an average 18.1% per year, foreign stocks returned 22.8% per year, corporate bonds returned about 11.6% per year, U.S. Treasury Bills averaged 8.9% per year, and large real estate investment pools averaged about 10.5% per year.

Average annual returns for some of these investment for 20 years are considerably lower; United States equities generated returns of about 13%, corporate bonds a little over 9% and treasury bills about 8%.

And if we take an extremely long 90 year look at United States investments, equities returns averaged about 10%, bonds about 5%, and treasury bills 4%. During the 90 year period, inflation averaged 3.2% per year.

I believe we should recognize a few points from these statistics. First, history strongly suggests that equities will probably not continue to generate the returns of the 1980's. Second, equities have historically surpassed all other traditional marketable securities in their return to the investor. This is even more important when we recognize that much of the equity return is deferred for tax payment purposes until the equities are actually sold. And my final point is that investment returns are not at heights that might be perceived, if you only pay attention to some of the extremes that we all read about from time to time. In particular, the gaudy returns generated by some real estate developers (not investors) in the early 1980's are not likely to be achieved by most of us. Perhaps that's not so bad considering that many of these returns were given back when real estate values dropped significantly.

DETERMINATION OF INVESTIBLE ASSETS

This may sound very elementary to those with financial or investment backgrounds, but a basic first step in the investment process of professionals is to understand exactly how much they have available to invest and to have some idea of how long they will have it, before it is needed for other purposes. A corporate pension fund may be in excellent shape today, but the picture might change dramatically in 5 years if the company has a large group of high paid employees on the verge of retirement and ready to take lump sum pensions. The pension funds need to be looked at from the standpoint of both present and future cash flow needs.

This step is no less important for individuals. If you have not spelled out your current financial position and some idea of future projections, at least in a rough form, it will be extremely difficult for you to make intelligent investment decisions.

As a simple example, let's consider an individual who receives a severance from his employer equal to one year's salary. Is this money available for an investment that carries risk or can tolerate a prolonged downturn in value? Possibly. If the person is wealthy or has a considerable cash reserve, it may be appropriate to use the money for investment that carries risk. On the other hand, if the person has a family to support, and limited prospects for a new job, investing this money beyond a simple interest bearing deposit might be very foolish. The only sure way to understand your financial situation is to lay it out in logical detail. It is not a difficult process and can be accomplished with a few hours of your devoted attention. For some, getting a little outside financial help to do this might be appropriate.

UNDERSTANDING AVAILABLE OPTIONS

It is critical that investors understand what types of investments are available to them. It is even more important that this menu of available choices be reduced to a small number of choices that the investor understands.

Most professional investment managers limit their investment horizon. In the United States, managers typically specialize in managing either stocks, bonds, cash equivalents (e.g.; money market funds) real estate, or commodities. In many cases, managers will even more narrowly specialize into such choices as value stocks, growth stocks, junk bonds, government bonds, industrial real estate, or apartment buildings to name a few.

Isn't it interesting that professional investors tend to specialize while individuals frequently will make their own individual investment choices in several of these categories.

Stocks or equities are a popular investment choice because they are usually highly liquid and over the long term have proven to generate a consistent high return to the investor. This is not to say that equities have not had some extended periods of inadequate returns. But since the end of World War II, equities have avoided a lengthy poor period such as occurred during the 1929 market crash and the depression of the 1930's.

As financial markets have developed around the world, equity investment choices should no longer be viewed as strictly United States. Countries such as Canada, Japan, and the United Kingdom have well developed stock markets. Many other countries in Latin America, the far east, and eastern Europe have developing markets. Limiting your investment horizon to only the United States may limit your ability to optimize your investment return. This seems particularly true as the United States moves towards a more mature industrialization status while other countries take our place with faster growing developing economies.

Bonds and other long term debt instruments are another popular investment choice because of their liquidity and perceived high returns to the investor. The investment possibilities include U.S. treasury bonds and notes, foreign government obligations, corporate bonds, bank certificates of deposit, and state and municipal obligations.

The money market which has developed since the 1970's provides another popular investment choice. It has allowed us to put our money in a highly liquid "cash equivalent" funds and to earn a return which frequently exceeds returns on bank savings accounts. Some of these investments are government or government insured and risk can be low or non-existent.

Real estate is another investment choice. Those of us who have owned property in many parts of the United States in the 1980's can attest to the high returns that real estate can generate. Available real estate choices to investors include second homes, real estate investment trusts, and real estate partnerships.

Other investments available to individual investors include commodities such as precious metals (gold, silver, etc.) collectibles (art, coins, etc.) and various venture funds. These investments are frequently not very liquid, carry high commissions, and require considerable expertise to understand them and achieve good results. I strongly urge you to avoid them unless you have this expertise or are willing to devote a significant amount of time in learning the subject.

How does the individual know where to locate all of the investment options available to him let alone know how to choose those most appropriate for investing? I feel that the *Wall Street Journal* is an excellent source for identifying investment markets. My feeling is that if an investment market is not listed in the *Journal*, it probably is a market that I'm better off avoiding.

Just what is in the *Journal*? First a variety of stock markets listings such as the New York Stock Exchange, the American Stock Exchange, the NASDAQ (over the counter listings), and several regional and overseas markets. Also reported are equity mutual funds and options markets.

The *Journal* reports a variety of bond markets including the New York and American exchanges and government bond quotes. It also includes bond mutual funds.

Commodity markets are reported as are money market rates and money market mutual funds. In addition, the *Journal* reports foreign exchange rates and currency trading data for those involved in foreign investing.

There are probably other financial publications as inclusive as the *Wall Street Journal*. By all means, use them if you are more comfortable with them. The point is to limit your investment horizon to those markets and securities that are reported in reputable financial publications. If you don't, you run the risk of holding investments which may or may not be saleable or which require particular expertise to be a successful investor.

UNDERSTANDING INVESTMENT RISK

An understanding of the concept of risk and reward is a very important ingredient for investing. As an investor, your objective should be to achieve the highest returns available, consistent with the amount of risk you are willing and able to tolerate.

What do we mean by risk? I define risk as the potential for permanent or temporary decline in the value of an investment. Professionals seem to deal with the risk issue in three ways; quality, market timing, and diversification.

Quality is simply investing in those things which have little or no chance of permanently losing their value. Short term bank deposits guaranteed by the U.S. government and U.S. Treasury bills are extremely low risk investments. There is virtually no chance for a permanent decline in value. However, these instruments offer low rates of return, the price you must pay for low or no risk.

Long term government bonds are high quality instruments with no risk of loss of principle. However, bonds change in value as interest rates move, so temporary changes in market value are not only possible but, in fact, occur daily.

Corporate equities and bonds carry varying degrees of risk depending on the quality of the company issuing the particular instruments. In addition, they have the risk of depreciating due to the external economic factors which impact the underlying businesses. We are all aware of the losses caused by investing in some of the poorer "junk bonds" issued in the 1980's. And we have all seen the effect of bankruptcies on equity holders.

Real estate, commodities and precious metals carry risk based on the quality of the investment, the price paid relative to actual intrinsic value, and the various economic factors which impact these investment categories.

It is important to consider quality in your investment decision process. Unless you are a sophisticated investor, investments which carry risk of significant and perhaps permanent loss of principle are best left to those who specialize in high risk, high reward types of investments.

Market timing is another way to try to minimize risk. No question about it, market timing works. If you can time your transactions to buy when prices are low and sell when prices are high, you're going to be a successful investor. The "sixty four dollar problem", of course, is to know when a price is high or low.

I am convinced that no-one has a meaningful and proven formula for short term market timing. But many investment managers, financial planners, and brokers will profess to have knowledge that a market or a particular investment is about to move up or down. I caution you to vigorously avoid most short term market timing investment advice. Most professionals I have known state emphatically that it can't be done.

Timing long term market moves is a different situation. For example, there is evidence to suggest that equity markets perform well in periods of low to moderate inflation (i.e. mid to late 1980's). On the contrary, equity markets have not done well in most high inflation periods (i.e. mid 1970's to early 1980's) or periods of deflation (i.e. 1930's).

There is evidence to suggest that equity markets perform well when interest rates are low or when expectations are that rates will go down. Bonds will normally do poorly when long term interest rates are expected to rise.

The final and, in my view, most important tool for managing investment risk is diversification. There is little chance that even the most astute investment professional will not make some investments which turn out poorly. The secret is to have enough investments so that the combination of the good and bad will give a satisfactory return.

Let's look at an example of the importance of diversification. Most of us are aware that IBM is a large, powerful corporation with an extremely strong balance sheet and , most important, an outstanding product line. As equity investing goes, putting all of your equity money in IBM in 1985 may have seemed prudent, but it would have been the extreme in non- diversification. The opposite in terms of diversification would have been to invest in every stock in an equity market, including many which would be considered absolutely horrible companies to own.

For the last 5 years of the 1980's, IBM stock actually declined significantly in value for it's shareholders (and continued to do so into the early 1990's), while an investment in all of the Standard and Poors 500 stocks, both good and bad, generated a compound return of about 12%.

A *Wall Street Journal* article of October 19, 1990 reported the results of a personal finance survey on diversification. It showed that, in the equity category, 10% of individuals own only one stock and 59% own 10 or fewer. These statistics reflect poor diversification. Most professionally invested portfolios include 30 securities or more.

The same message applies to other types of investments. Investing in one "junk" bond carries the extreme risk that the issuer may default, while investing in a portfolio of many "junk" bonds carries a very low risk that all will default. And real estate is no different. Owning one property is usually considered much riskier than owning all or a piece of a pool of properties. My personal rule of thumb is to avoid holding more than 5% of assets in any single investment.

To summarize, professionals use quality, market timing, and diversification to reduce investment risk. Individuals are well served to diversify. Quality investments cannot be argued against but recognize that low risk usually results in low returns. Short term market timing is a game best left to others. Timing long term market moves has some merit and will be discussed later on.

UNDERSTANDING RISK TOLERANCE

We've discussed the importance of investment risk as it relates to the types of investments you might wish to consider. However, you cannot make your investment decisions until you have determined how much risk you, as an individual, can tolerate.

A poorly funded pension fund with high annual requirements for retiree payments must consider it's condition before deciding how much to allocate to stocks, bonds, cash reserve, etc. More than likely, the manager of this fund will have a lower risk portfolio than a fund which is very well funded and has negligible current cash needs.

To put this subject in an individual's perspective, let's look at three fictitious people. Worker A earns $40,000 per year, is 37 years old, is married, and has two children in their mid-teens. The family has a net worth of about $100,000, 50% in the equity in their home and 50% in savings earmarked mostly for their children's educations. I would view this family as having a very low risk tolerance because of the need to maintain an emergency reserve as well as to have funds available for tuition payments in a few years. The family's finances can not tolerate a lengthy decline in the stock or bond markets, and therefore should use considerable caution in using these markets.

Manager B makes $100,000 per year, is 55 years old, has a spouse and adult children, and has a net worth of about $600,000. The net worth is split about equally between equity in a home, pension and other retirement assets, and a variety of stocks, bonds, and cash investments.

This couple is getting positioned for retirement but has several years left to accumulate assets. I would consider them worthy of moderate investment risk. They could tolerate a lengthy, temporary decline in the value of their investments.

Executive C earns $500,000 per year in a flourishing self-owned business, is 40 years old, and has a spouse who is also a high earner. They have a net worth in excess of $2 million consisting of equity in two homes and investments. Obviously, this couple is in a position to take on much greater investment risk than either Worker A or Manager B.

The process of measuring investment risk tolerance is an extremely important part of the investment process. It involves examining the following critical issues, each of which will be discussed at greater length later on:

- age and life stage
- income
- net worth
- future cash needs
- retirement plans
- income expectations
- values of existing assets
- contingencies

This list is not too unlike one you might see in an investment planners arsenal. The problem that we pointed out earlier is that most investment planners have a single objective of selling you their products. These products are frequently not the ones which will generate good returns and frequently are accompanied by extremely high up-front commissions.

Invest Like The Successful Pros

DO PROFESSIONALS REALLY PERFORM WELL

Do professionals really have all of the investment answers? If so, why aren't they enjoying their wealth on the French Riviera instead of managing other peoples money or selling investment advice?

The simple answer is that all professional investment managers and sponsors are not successful. In fact, I believe that most are not successful, using the criterion that success means beating the average of the universe in which you invest.

Let's look at how professional investors did in the 1980's. For the 10 years, the Standard and Poors 500 stock index returned a compound average of 18.1% to it's investors. The S&P 500 is an index composite of the largest publicly owned U.S. companies. The broader Wilshire 5000 stock index, which includes both large and small companies, averaged a compound return of 16.6%. These returns. I believe, represent reasonable targets for investment managers to exceed or at least equal after deducting all fees. If not, why not simply invest your money in an index fund?

How did the pro's do in the same 10 year period? The median return for a universe of 337 equity funds of banks and insurance companies was 16.7% *. These returns are inclusive of transaction costs but not management fees. Management fees typically run one-half to two percent of assets under management. It's easy to see that these averages neither exceeded nor even equalled the S&P or Wilshire indices for the 10 year period.

*PENSIONS AND INVESTMENTS PERFORMANCE EVALUATION REPORT, December 31, 1990, Pensions & Investments, Rogers, Casey

How can this be? If the premise is correct that professionals outperform individual investors, and the average professional can't even achieve market averages, is it any wonder why the individual is confused and has moved away from the stock market?

The solution, of course, is to invest in a way that you can avoid the below average performers and find the superior performers. Can it be done? If we know that the average manager slightly underperforms the averages, perhaps 40% or so are outperforming in any given year. The secret then is to figure out how to identify this 40% group in advance.

Before we assume that this is an easy task, let me refer to a study conducted by Wyatt Asset Services, a subsidiary of The Wyatt Company,* a prestigious international actuarial and financial consulting firm. This study analyzed the investment performance of 410 large institutional equity market funds for two periods, (1980-84 and 1985-89). For each period, each manager's performance was categorized as super (greater than 120% of S&P 500 performance), high (110%-120% of the S&P), market (95%-110% of the S&P), substandard (80%-95% of the S&P), and poor (less than 80% of the S&P). The results of this study are summarized as follows:

-for 1980-84, 30% of the funds generated super or high returns, 20% generated market returns, and 50% generated substandard or poor returns.
-in the 1985-89 period, only 2% of the funds performed in the super or high categories, while 85% were either substandard or poor performers or dropped out of the universe (probably the worst performers of the group)

* INVESTMENT INSIGHTS, Volume 2, Number 2, August 1990,   Wyatt Asset Services Inc.

- most of the funds improving their performance were in the lower brackets in 1980-84 and most of the funds with poorer 1985-89 performance were in better brackets in the 1980-84 period.
- only 4 funds (less than 1% of the universe) were super or high performers in both 5 year periods.

What do the combination of the PIPER and Wyatt studies seem to tell us? First, they suggest that we have about a 40%-50% likelihood of picking a professional investment manager who will perform above the market average in a given year. Second, if we find a manager who outperforms for us, there is less than a 50% probability that he will continue to outperform. Past performance does not seem to be a reliable indicator of how a manager will perform in the future.

Is it totally impossible to win as an investor? Hopefully we'll convince you that you can invest in a way in which you can achieve returns, after all fees and expenses, that are better than the average professional.

WHO'S ADVICE SHOULD YOU ACCEPT

Investment advice can come from many places. The world seems to have an oversupply of experts in economics, politics, and investing. With so many sources of investment advice, who should we listen to?

Let's start with our friends and associates. How many of them have given you tales of their great investment victories? And since they seldom talk about their failed investments, they musn't have any. Should we pay heed to their "hot tips"? Not me!

What about brokers - stock, real estate, commodities, etc? If they are in the investment business, they must know more than me about investing.

Don't automatically conclude that brokers are knowledgeable about investing - they may simply know more than you do about selling investments and closing sales transactions. Brokers are in business to earn commissions. Their livelihood depends on transactions, not on whether their recommendations turn out to be right or wrong. Should you take the advice of brokers? Absolutely not, unless they can provide you with an independently verified record of successful investment results over a long period of time. I have yet to find a broker meeting this qualification.

Should we let the media guide our investment decisions? Another dangerous practice. Investments gain most media attention at the extremes, and the indication given is frequently the opposite of what is likely to happen.

When the Dow Jones Industrials reached 3000 in July 1990 it got very positive attention, suggesting that the stock market was still on a positive roll. It turned out to be the perfect time to sell equities. Conversely, the media was all "doom and gloom" after the stock market crash of October 1987, and yet this was the perfect time to buy equities. The same euphoria existed for northeast real estate at it's 1986-87 peak and gold when it went over $800 per ounce in the 1970's. Probably the most reliance that should be put on media headlines is that of a negative indicator.

Investment newsletters, investment counselors, and financial planners are other sources, In my view, they get about the same rating as brokers. Unless they can provide you with an independently verified history of successful investing, I caution you to avoid their advice.

Let's think about investment newsletters. If they really had outstanding investment advice to give, all of the newsletter and Wall Street insiders would probably have access to this advice long before you even saw it, let alone had time to react. The reason this doesn't seem to happen is probably because newsletter tips are generally not considered worthwhile, even though some of the individual recommendations may be quite good from time to time.

Financial planners are a very questionable source for good investment advice. A university finance professor and former research director for the United States Controller of the Currency, was quoted in 1990 in the New Britain (CT)) Herald expressing his opinion that perhaps 99% of financial planners dispense bad advice. My guess is that the opinion is essentially correct and that financial planners provide no better investment advice than brokers.

In my view, a greater problem with financial planners is that they frequently sell products with very high commission rates. And the only thing that high commissions usually means is that you end with an investment that takes an extraordinary return in order for you to achieve a reasonable return on your money. For example, lets say you make an investment in rare coins and the sales commission is 30% (a figure I believe to be what is often charged). In order for you to just break even, you need a return of almost 46%. How long might that take? And what about any profit on your investment?

Now that I've opined that you shouldn't rely on brokers, financial planners, friends, investment newsletters, or the media for investment advice, who should you rely on? I believe the answer is yourself, and hopefully I can convince you.

CONCLUSION

This book is intended to help you find a process to successfully manage your investments. There are many things that you can do wrong, but following are what I consider the 10 most significant investment "sins", all of which I hope this book will help you avoid:

- having unrealistic expectations
- not establishing objectives
- not understanding risk
- not determining your investible assets
- accepting poor advice
- trying to time market moves
- not diversifying
- not cost averaging
- not monitoring results
- having no "sell discipline"

CHAPTER II

*Investment Choices
and
Expected Returns*

CHAPTER II

INVESTMENT CHOICES AND EXPECTED RETURNS

INVESTMENT CATEGORIES

There are a considerable variety of investments available to the individual investor. Some are very appropriate to consider while others, I believe, are quite inappropriate because of the risks and uncertainty that go along with them. Without question, any discussion of investing needs to identify the investments suitable for each particular investor.

CASH EQUIVALENTS:

This category of investing is undoubtedly the most popular. Cash equivalents reflect indebtedness of the issuers and include bank savings accounts, U.S. government treasury bills, and a variety of money market funds that are available through banks and other financial institutions. The investment instruments are short term in nature and the investment returns or interest rates paid are reflective of short term interest rate markets.

Issuers of cash equivalents range from individual banks and thrift institutions to brokerage firms to the U.S. government. Cash equivalents do not fluctuate in market value and have lives of one year or less at which time they mature or interest rates are revised to current market levels.

BONDS:

Bonds, like cash equivalents, are securities which evidence indebtedness. They are issued by governments and corporations to finance their various activities. Bonds have life spans that range from one year to more than 30 years and typically pay fixed rates of interest. Shorter life securities of this nature are frequently classified as notes rather than bonds, but the same characteristics apply.

Bonds range in quality from that of the U.S. government to "junk" securities which reflect the indebtedness of corporations with questionable ability to repay. Bonds vary in market price based on interest rate movements and expectations as well as issuer financial quality and financial ratings set by rating agencies such as Standard & Poors and Moody's Investors Services.

Bonds and notes available to U.S. investors include foreign as well as domestic instruments.

EQUITIES:

Equities or stocks are securities which represent an ownership interest in a business. Investments can be in foreign or domestic companies. Equities can be in the form of common stocks (by far the most typical), as well as preferred or convertible stocks, both of which have characteristics similar to both bonds and common stocks.

The market value of an equity moves based on changes in economic conditions as well as changes in the fortunes of the issuing company. Many stocks pay dividends to provide at least a partial return to investors. A major difference between stocks and bonds is that stock values are expected to increase as the issuing company increases in value while bonds are owned to get a fixed interest return only. Bond values can, however, fluctuate if ratings (by Moody's, Standard & Poors,etc.) change, as was demonstrated repeatedly in the 1980's as company's took on more and more debt.

REAL ESTATE:

Real estate, from an investing standpoint, can range from ownership of a second home to an interest in a pool of properties. Real estate values move based on changes in economic conditions of individual properties or the market. Real estate has traditionally provided returns somewhere between that of stocks and bonds.

The particular shortcomings of direct investing in specific properties are the absence of both a process to correctly value the investments and a liquid market to dispose of the investments at will. These shortcomings generally do not exist for stocks, bonds, and cash equivalents.

COLLECTIBLES:

Collectibles are another type of investment. They range from rare coins and works of art to simpler things like baseball cards. In my view, unless you have considerable expertise in a particular type of collectible, investment risk is substantial. There seems to be no other investment category based more on emotion and status than collectibles.

COMMODITIES:

Another investment alternative is commodities. Commodities can be in the form of farm products, precious metals, oil, and a variety of other things you can identify by reviewing the appropriate section of your financial newspaper. I view commodities as another category in which expertise is an appropriate requirement before investment should be considered. Commodities seem to me to be much more short term and speculative in nature rather than long term investments.

OTHER:

Undoubtedly there other things that fit the definition of investment candidates such as venture capital, timberlands, and a long list of products that are hybrids of the basic investments referred to in this chapter. I see no reason to consider them as appropriate candidates for your investment dollars unless you have particular expertise in them.

REALISTIC EXPECTATIONS

What returns should an investor expect to achieve? Understandably, what to expect as a return on any investment is of critical importance, otherwise, it is not possible to evaluate the risk you should take in making the investment.

As a general statement, higher risk should carry higher return potential and vice-versa. We will look at risk in greater detail later on. For now, lets take a more detailed view of the investment return history of equities, bonds, and cash equivalents, those investment categories that seem to be most relevant for most of us.

EQUITIES:

Table I details 63 years of equity market performance (dividends and appreciation) as measured by the Standard & Poors 500 universe of stocks, a well accepted measurement vehicle. The table reveals some interesting facts:

- Each decade yielded a positive return, varying from 5.4% in the 1930's to 20.8% in the 1980's.
- There was one period of 3 consecutive negative return years (1930, 1931, 1932) and 2 periods of 2 consecutive negative years (1940, 1941 and 1973,1974)
- There were 43 up-market years and 17 down years
- There were long periods of consecutive up years (8 years 1982-89 and 6 years 1947-52)
- It took almost 5 years to recover the losses incurred in the 1930-32 period (and until the 1940's to show an appreciable return) and about 3 years to recover the1973-74 losses.
- The arithmetic average long term nominal returns were 11.8% for the entire 63 year period and 13.8% for the 40 post-World War II years.

The most important message is that equities provide positive long term returns but not without the risk of prolonged down periods. This makes it of critical importance that investors have sufficient cash reserves to carry through these down periods without having to sell equities when prices are low.

TABLE I
STANDARD & POORS 500 STOCKS
INVESTMENT RETURN

Year	Return	Year	Return
1930	-24.2%	1960	0.4%
1931	-43.5	1961	26.9
1932	- 7.7	1962	- 8.7
1933	-52.8	1963	22.8
1934	0.0	1964	16.4
1935	47.3	1965	12.4
1936	33.3	1966	-10.0
1937	-35.2	1967	23.9
1938	31.4	1968	11.0
1939	0.0	1969	- 8.4
1930'S	5.4%	1960's	8.7%
1940	- 9.8%	1970	3.9%
1941	-12.0	1971	14.2
1942	20.5	1972	19.0
1943	25.0	1973	-14.7
1944	20.0	1974	-26.3
1945	36.4	1975	37.2
1946	- 8.3	1976	23.8
1947	6.1	1977	- 7.2
1948	5.1	1978	6.5
1949	18.5	1979	18.5
1940's	10.2%	1970's	7.5%
1950	31.7%	1980	32.5%
1951	24.0	1981	- 4.9
1952	18.0	1982	21.5
1953	- 1.0	1983	22.5
1954	52.4	1984	6.2
1955	31.4	1985	31.6
1956	6.5	1986	18.6
1957	-10.7	1987	5.2
1958	43.2	1988	16.5
1959	12.0	1989	31.6
1950's	20.8%	1980's	18.1%
1990	- 3.1%	**63 YEARS**	
1991	30.5%	**(1930 - 1992)**	**11.8%**
1992	7.6%		

TABLE II
STANDARD & POORS
AA BONDS INVESTMENT RETURN

Year	Return	Year	Return
1930	4.9%	1960	4.5%
1931	4.8	1961	4.5
1932	5.5	1962	4.4
1933	4.9	1963	4.4
1934	4.3	1964	4.5
1935	3.8	1965	4.5
1936	3.5	1966	5.2
1937	3.6	1967	5.7
1938	3.5	1968	6.3
1939	3.2	1969	7.2
1930's	4.2%	1960's	5.1%
1940	3.1%	1970	8.2%
1941	2.9	1971	7.6
1942	3.0	1972	7.6
1943	3.0	1973	7.7
1944	2.8	1974	8.4
1945	2.7	1975	8.9
1946	2.6	1976	8.6
1947	2.7	1977	8.3
1948	2.9	1978	8.9
1949	2.7	1979	9.8
1940's	2.8%	1970's	8.4%
1950	2.7%	1980	12.0%
1951	2.9	1981	14.3
1952	3.0	1982	13.7
1953	3.3	1983	11.9
1954	3.0	1984	12.0
1955	3.1	1985	10.1
1956	3.5	1986	9.4
1957	4.1	1987	9.7
1958	3.9	1988	9.9
1959	4.5	1989	12.8
1950'S	3.4%	1980's	11.6%
1990	9.2%	**63 YEARS**	
1991	14.6	**(1930 - 1992)**	**6.1%**
1992	7.6%		

BONDS:

Table II details 63 years of bond returns (interest and appreciation) as reflected by the Standard & Poors Bond Index of companies with AA (high quality) financial ratings. This table also reveals some interesting facts:

- Bond returns have been positive for every decade, ranging from 2.8% in the 1940's to 11.6% in the 1980's.
- There has been no year of negative return
- In 23 of the 63 year period, bond returns exceeded equity returns reflected in Table I.

What message do we get from this data? Bonds always generate positive returns and therefore can be viewed as less risky than equities. But the long term returns from bonds is lower than that of equities.

CASH EQUIVALENTS:

Table III details 63 years of cash returns as represented by the average annual returns from U.S. treasury bills, a common cash equivalent measurement. The table reveals the following data:

- Cash returns have not been negative in any year. This is not surprising since it would require negative interest rates for it to happen. As you can see, however, there have been years of zero or negligible returns.
- In no year did cash generate a higher return than bonds although cash can and does exceed the negative returns of stocks in down markets.

TABLE III
UNITED STATES TREASURY BILLS
INVESTMENT RETURN

1930	2.2%	1960	2.9%
1931	1.4	1961	2.4
1932	0.9	1962	2.8
1933	0.5	1963	3.2
1934	0.3	1964	3.6
1935	0.1	1965	4.0
1936	0.1	1966	4.9
1937	0.5	1967	4.3
1938	0.1	1968	5.3
1939	0.0	1969	6.7
1930's	0.6%	1960's	4.0%
1940	0.0%	1970	6.4%
1941	0.1	1971	4.3
1942	0.3	1972	4.1
1943	0.4	1973	7.0
1944	0.4	1974	7.9
1945	0.4	1975	5.8
1946	0.4	1976	5.0
1947	0.6	1977	5.3
1948	1.0	1978	7.2
1949	1.1	1979	10.1
1940's	0.5%	1970's	6.3%
1950	1.2%	1980	11.6%
1951	1.6	1981	14.0
1952	1.8	1982	10.5
1953	1.9	1983	8.6
1954	1.0	1984	9.4
1955	1.7	1985	7.3
1956	2.7	1986	5.9
1957	3.3	1987	5.8
1958	1.8	1988	6.7
1959	3.4	1989	8.9
1950'S	2.0%	1980's	8.9%
1990	8.3%	**63 YEARS**	
1991	6.3	**(1930 - 1992)**	**3.8%**
1992	3.5%		

TABLE IV
UNITED STATES INFLATION
INVESTMENT RETURN

1930	- 2.7%%	1960	1.6%
1931	- 8.0	1961	1.0
1932	-11.5	1962	2.2
1933	- 2.6	1963	1.6
1934	8.9	1964	1.5
1935	2.5	1965	2.7
1936	0.0	1966	3.8
1937	4.8	1967	2.6
1938	- 1.5	1968	5.0
1939	- 1.6	1969	- 5.6
1930'S	-1.2%	1960's	2.7%
1940	2.4%	1970	5.5%
1941	6.2	1971	5.7
1942	6.5	1972	4.7
1943	2.7	1973	6.5
1944	1.3	1974	9.1
1945	2.6	1975	9.8
1946	23.6	1976	6.4
1947	13.9	1977	6.7
1948	6.8	1978	7.3
1949	- 4.0	1979	8.9
1940'S	6.2%	1970's	7.1%
1950	1.7%	1980	9.0%
1951	5.0	1981	9.7
1952	1.6	1982	6.4
1953	1.6	1983	3.9
1954	1.5	1984	3.7
1955	3.4	1985	3.0
1956	3.3	1986	2.7
1957	3.6	1987	3.3
1958	2.1	1988	3.4
1959	2.4	1989	4.8
1950'S	2.6%	1980's	5.0%
1990	6.2%	**63 YEARS**	
1991	3.1	**(1930 - 1992)**	**3.8%**
1992	3.0%		

INFLATION:

Table IV reflects inflation over the same 63 year period and is included here for the purpose of helping measure the true value of the returns reflected in Tables I, II, and III.

Historical returns for other investment classes are difficult to determine with accuracy. Real estate is generally considered to provide a return somewhere between equities and bonds, but, of course, carries the burden of liquidity risk. Commodities can vary significantly in return, depending on the particular commodity in question. Collectibles also vary dramatically depending on the particular item, plus carry the heavy burden of very high commissions.

CONCLUSIONS:

What conclusions can we reach in looking at these tables in combination with each other?

- Achieving a "real" return should be one of your principal objectives. "Real" return is defined as nominal or reported return less inflation. Without question, equities have provided the superior "real" return as is shown in the following summary:

REAL INVESTMENT RETURN

	EQUITIES	BONDS	CASH
1930's	6.6%	5.4%	1.8%
1940's	4.0%	-3.4%	-5.7%
1950's	18.2%	0.8%	-0.6%
1960's	6.0%	2.4%	1.3%
1970's	0.4%	1.3%	-0.9%
1980's	13.0%	6.6%	3.9%
60 YEARS	8.1%	2.2%	-0.1%

- Equity values are also the most volatile of the three in
vestment classes. Therefore, investments should not be
held in equities with any funds which will be needed for
other purposes within the next several, perhaps as
many as 5, years.

- bonds provide a greater return than cash equivalents,
but bear in mind that bonds are subject to price volatility
while cash is not. A prudent rule of thumb might be to not
hold funds in bond investments if it is anticipated that
the bonds will have to be sold over the next 2 years.

We have identified cash equivalents (interest bearing
bank deposits, treasury bills, money market funds), bonds
and notes issued by the U.S. government and U.S. corporations, and equities issued by U.S. corporations as appropriate investment vehicles for individual investors. I also believe that a small percent in real estate and foreign stocks
are appropriate for some investors.

How do these choices compare to professionally managed

funds? They are essentially the same. Wells Fargo Nikko Investment Advisors * , for example recommends the following asset mix for it's very large client base:

- 48% equities of which about 2% are foreign

- 45% bonds of which 2% are foreign. Of the 43% U.S. bonds, 23% are government and 20% are corporate or real estate-related securities.

- 7% cash equivalents.

This asset mix is certainly substantiated by the fact that stocks, bonds, and cash equivalents, in total, represent a large percentage of securities markets.

While there is no mention of real estate ownership in the Wells allocation, in my experience, many pension and endowment funds have assets allocated to real estate and the amount is usually less than 15% of total assets.

As another indicator, the following asset mix was reported in a 1991 study of corporate defined benefit plans *:

Equities (no domestic/international split)	49%
Bonds and other fixed income	36%
Real estate	5%
Cash & other	10%

As this chapter suggests, there are many investment choices available. But the decisions as to which are best for you cannot be made without examining both the risk factors which accompany each investment category and your individual tolerance to absorb risk. these issues will be dealt with in the next few chapters.

Chapter III

Investment Risk

CHAPTER III

INVESTMENT RISK

Chapter II discussed the various available investment choices. Those focused on as being appropriate for most United States investors included U.S. cash equivalents, U.S. government and corporate bonds, U.S. and foreign stocks, and perhaps real estate. Commodities and collectibles were discussed as not being appropriate for most people.

RISK FACTORS

After identifying the available categories of investment, a very critical question then is how much risk each investment carries. Investment risk is defined as the possibility of permanent or temporary loss in value. Investment risk takes several forms and we will discuss those that seem to be most critical.

MARKET RISK:

Each investment you make is part of a broader market. This can be a stock market such as the New York Stock Exchange or a less formal market such as residential real estate in Los Angeles. I view market risk as the potential that a market will suffer a permanent decline in value. Gold reached $800 an ounce in the 1970's and has not approached anything close to that level since. Those owning gold at it's peak have suffered greatly from the market risk associated with the commodity.

The 63 year investment return figures in Chapter II, I believe, are convincing arguments that there is no market risk associated with major U.S.stock, bond, and U.S. treasury bill markets. The major bond and treasury bill markets have no history of decline. The major U.S. stock market has a history of temporary declines always followed by even greater periods of increase in value.

CREDIT RISK:

Credit or security risk is simply the possibility that your particular investment performs badly, despite the fact that the market in which it resides may perform well. The U.S. stock market performed well through the 1982-90 bull market and yet New England regional banks were terrible investments as they suffered tremendous real estate writeoffs resulting from the valuation excesses of the 1980's. The solution to credit risk is diversification. If you own a broad selection of investments, you can eliminate the harm that might be caused by poor performance of one or a few of them because your selection will include others which will perform above the norm. Credit risk is the risk that most individual investors don't pay attention to and generally suffer the most from, and yet it seems to be the easiest to avoid.

LIQUIDITY RISK:

Another important risk to consider is liquidity risk. Despite a presumed value of an asset, this value is meaningful only if can be converted to cash. You may have owned a fine commercial building in Texas in 1982, but your ability to turn this asset into cash was very low as Texas properties fell dramatically in value and the inventory of unsold properties reached historic highs.

CURRENCY RISK:

Currency risk exists if your investments are foreign currencies or are denominated in foreign currencies. You may own stock in a Japanese company which is performing tremendously, but if the value of the Japanese Yen is declining against the U.S. Dollar, your appreciation may disappear. You have suffered from the currency risk associated with having your investment denominated Yen rather than Dollars.

VOLATILITY RISK:

Volatility is a risk that exists for all but cash equivalent investments. It is the risk associated with the continual fluctuations of free markets. Volatility risk is temporary in nature while market risk, which we discussed earlier, is permanent or very long term in nature. The stock market crash of October 1987 clearly demonstrated the volatility of stock markets. It is a good example of the risk of being invested in a market that is subject to both economic conditions as well as the emotions of it's investors. Volatility is the most difficult risk for the individual to have to deal with as we will discuss later on.

In the investment world, the term for volatility risk is standard deviation. It is a measurement of how much a return varies from the average return.

The May 20, 1991 issue of Barron's* showed some (volatility) risk and (investment) return data prepared by the investment banking firm of Morgan Stanley. Following are some extracts for the 50 years 1940-90:

	ANNUAL RETURN	VOLATILITY (standard deviation)
Japanese equities	15.7%	29.2%
S&P 500 equities	11.6%	15.1%
Commercial real estate	7.5%	4.9%
U.S. government bonds	4.5%	9.4%
Treasury bills	4.4%	3.4%
Inflation	4.6%	3.9%

This data shows that Japanese equities have generated an average return over the 50 year period of 15.7%. However, the volatility of 29.2% indicates that, in most periods, the return ranged from a negative 13.5% (the 15.7% average less the 29.2% volatility factor) to plus 44.9% (the 15.7% average plus the 29.2% volatility factor). The message is clear for both Japanese and U.S. equities: average long term equity returns are achievable, but it is critical to have liquidity available to carry you through significant market swings. On the other end of the spectrum, you can avoid significant swings by investing in low volatility treasury bills, but in doing so, you must sacrifice investment return.

RISK MEASUREMENT

Identifying risk is only valuable if it can be used to improving investment results. I have developed the follow-

*CONSIDER THE ALTERNATIVES, Barrons, May 20, 1991

ing risk matrix to help understand the risk measurement process.

I have excluded foreign cash and bond markets as well as foreign real estate. The opportunity to achieve U.S. dollar returns above that of comparable U.S. investments is not, in my opinion, sufficient to justify taking the currency risk associated with foreign investments.

| | —————RISK————— | | | | |
	MARKET	CREDIT	LIQUIDITY	CURRENCY	VOLATILITY
CASH EQUIV.	LOW	MOD.	NONE	NONE	NONE
U.S.BONDS	LOW	HIGH	NONE	NONE	HIGH
U.S. STOCKS	LOW	HIGH	NONE	NONE	HIGH
FOREIGN STOCKS	LOW	HIGH	NONE	HIGH	HIGH
REAL ESTATE	MOD.	HIGH	HIGH	NONE	HIGH
COMMODITIES	MOD.	HIGH	NONE	NONE	HIGH
COLLECTIBLES	HIGH	HIGH	HIGH	VARIES	HIGH

Market risk is considered low for all but certain real estate and commodities as well as collectibles because we start with the premise that only major cash, bond, stock, and commodities markets are in our investment horizon. We cannot ignore, however, the possibility that some real estate or commodities markets might decline and not come back or that collectibles might fall out of favor for indefinite periods of time.

On the other hand, until it is managed, there is considerable credit risk in every in each of our investment categories. This is even true in the cash equivalent category given the possibility of having uninsured funds with a troubled bank.

Again, given the assumption of major liquid markets, only real estate and collectibles have liquidity risk, that is the inability to have an available buyer for your asset if you want to sell it. Cash, stocks, bonds and commodities have sophisticated markets which, in most situations, provide buyers for all sellers.

Foreign stocks have currency risk, that is, the possibility of losing investment value strictly because of decline in one or more currency exchange rates. Collectibles may or may not carry this risk.

For all intents and purposes, cash is the only investment choice having no volatility risk, that is, risk of a temporary decline in the value of an asset. All other classes have moderate to high risk. For stocks in particular, this was clearly demonstrated in the 63 year performance data in Chapter II.

I believe the secret to being a successful investor is to manage the risk process such that you minimize as many risks as possible without being so cautious that you forego investment return. The steps in this process are as follows:

- Avoid investments with high market risk including commodities and collectibles, since most of us know little about them or what drives their values. And stay away from securities markets in which there is any question that you may not find a ready buyer for your investment. An example would be investing in the "penny stock" arena which caused many to incur significant losses at different times in the past.

- Avoid, or at least minimize investments which carry liquidity or currency risk. I think it is reasonable for most people to not have more than 10% of their investments in real estate and 10% in foreign stocks.

- Be cognizant of volatility risk. We will deal with it more when we discuss the merging of investment and individual risk.

- Above all else, hold a diversified portfolio of investments as the single best way to minimize, if not eliminate, credit risk.

If I redo the risk matrix under the assumption of a managed risk strategy, including portfolio diversification, it now looks like the following:

————————RISK————————

	MARKET	CREDIT	LIQUIDITY	CURRENCY	VOLATILITY
CASH EQUIV.	LOW	LOW	NONE	NONE	MOD.
U.S.BONDS	LOW	LOW	NONE	NONE	HIGH
U.S. STOCKS	LOW	LOW	NONE	NONE	HIGH
FOREIGN STOCKS	LOW	LOW	NONE	HIGH	HIGH
REAL ESTATE	MOD.	LOW	HIGH'	NONE	HIGH

What have we accomplished so far? We have eliminated those investments carrying high market risk namely commodities and collectibles.

We have reduced individual security credit risk with portfolio diversification.

We are now left with the following choices:

- Cash equivalents with low or no risk in all categories. Cash then represents the safest investment choice and is appropriate even for the investor who can handle virtually no risk. The only safer option, I guess, is to put your savings under your mattress.

- U.S. bonds, with low or no risk in all categories except volatility in which there is moderate risk. U.S. bonds, then, are a safe investment category if you have adequate cash reserve to carry you through periods when your bond principal may have temporarily declined in market value.

- U.S. stocks, with low or no risk in all categories except volatility where they carry a high risk. Again, this is a safe investment category if you have adequate cash reserve to carry you through periods in which your stock portfolio may be in a lengthy, albeit temporary decline in market value.

- foreign stocks which have a different risk profile than US stocks. While they also are low in market, liquidity, and credit risk, and high in volatility risk, they also carry high currency risk. If the U.S. dollar strengthens against the currency in which your foreign stocks are denominated, you may lose on your investment even if the stocks do well in their own currencies. For this reason, I do not advise putting more than 10% of investible assets in foreign equities.

- Real estate, which also carries a different risk profile than all other choices because real estate almost always carries high liquidity risk. You can sell stocks (foreign or domestic), bonds, and cash equivalents whenever you want. You can only sell real estate if a buyer comes forth with an offer. For this very important reason, I believe most investment portfolios should have no more than 10% in real estate.

CHAPTER IV

Determine Your Investible Assets

CHAPTER IV

DETERMINE YOUR INVESTIBLE ASSETS

THE IMPORTANCE OF FINANCIAL STATEMENTS

Financial statements are the critical tool in measuring business performance. They are prepared at least quarterly and usually monthly. Without them, businesses would find it difficult, if not impossible to know their financial strength, whether they are progressing or regressing as a business, and how they are performing relative to competition. Also, financial statements help determine the financing needs of businesses and are critical to income tax and other compliance requirements.

Financial statements are also important for individuals and particularly individual investors. One of the first things you should do to begin the process of investing like a professional is to determine your investible assets. Do you really have assets available for discretionary investing? Or have all of your assets been earmarked for other near-term needs such as tuition payments or loan repayments?

A carefully constructed financial position or personal balance sheet should be prepared as the basepoint for your investment process. It differs from a business balance sheet only in asset and liability terminology and perhaps format.

FORMAT

The accounting format traditionally used by the financial

world to lay out a balance sheet is a very appropriate one and should be used if you are comfortable with it. It looks like the following:

ASSETS		LIABILITIES	
Current	x x x	Current	x x x
Non - current	x x x	Non-current	x x x
		NET WORTH	x x x

ASSETS = LIABILITIES + NET WORTH

All assets are in the left column. They are usually in order of ease in which they can be converted to cash with cash coming first and the least liquid asset coming last. Liabilities and net worth are in the right column. Double entry bookkeeping requires that total assets must equal the sum of liabilities (claims by creditors against the assets) plus net worth (claims by owners against the assets).

But if you are not totally wed to the business balance sheet format, or if you are looking for a format that may be easier to use and understand, I suggest the following:

	ASSETS	LIABILITIES	NET WORTH
Current	x x x	(x x x)	x x x
Permanent	x x x	(x x x)	x x x
Retirement	x x x	(x x x)	x x x
Investment	x x x	(x x x)	x x x

TOTAL ASSETS - LIABILITIES = NET WORTH

This format relates each asset with it's corresponding

liability, if any. For example, a home with a market value of $250,000 and a mortgage of $75,000 would be displayed as a $250,000 permanent asset and next to it a $75,000 liability, and next to it $175,000 of net worth. I believe this provides a much clearer identification of the sources of net worth and therefore is an easier balance sheet to manage and understand.

The next section utilizes this format in preparing financial statements for Worker A, Manager B, and Executive C, who were introduced in Chapter I. If you take the time to understand the format, it should not be difficult. If you are the type who just cannot deal with compiling financial data, I suggest you utilize an accountant or perhaps a friend or relative to help you prepare your personal balance sheet.

But please give this subject it's rightful allocation of time. There is no issue more important to you than identifying the assets you have available for investing. Without it, the investment process is significantly handicapped.

EXAMPLES

Table I is the balance sheet of Worker A. You will recall that Worker A is married, age 37, and has annual income of $40,000. The family has a mortgaged home, the usual assortment of family bills, and significant orthodontist bills on the horizon. The families assets include $40,000 in savings accounts and $25,000 in equity mutual funds.

Worker A's current assets begin with the cash and cash reserve category. But in fact, this figure should not be determined until all other current assets and liabilities have been identified.

TABLE I
WORKER A BALANCE SHEET

	ASSETS	LIABILITIES	NET WORTH
CURRENT			
Cash	$22,000	$0	$22,000
Accts Receivable	0	0	0
Amounts Owed	0	2,000	(2,000)
Anticipated Liabilities	0	17,000	(17,000)
Other	0	0	0
	22,000	19,000	3,000
PERMANENT			
Home & Mortgage	140,000	90,000	50,000
Autos & Auto Loans	12,000	7,000	5,000
Business Interests	0	0	0
Other	10,000	0	10,000
	162,000	97,000	65,000
RETIREMENT			
Vested Pension	5,000	0	5,000
IRA/Keough Accounts	0	0	0
Savings/401K Plan	0	0	0
Deferred Compensation	0	0	0
Other	0	0	0
	5,000	0	5,000
INVESTMENT			
Cash Reserve	11,000	0	11,000
Bonds	0	0	0
Stocks	25,000	0	25,000
Real Estate	0	0	0
Other	0	0	0
	36,000	0	36,000
TOTALS	$225,000	$116,000	**$109,000**

Amounts owed to others reflects amounts currently owed beyond normal household expenses. Normal household items are excluded since the family has income each month to meet these obligations. Other near-term obligations reflect the extraordinary amount which will be owed to the orthodontist within the year and the estimated cost of a used car the family expects to acquire soon. These liabilities total $19,000 and I have arbitrarily reflected a current cash need of $22,000 to handle payment of these liabilities and to provide an additional $3,000 reserve.

Permanent assets and liabilities are the next balance sheet category. The family owns a home with an estimated market value of $140,000 and a mortgage of $90,000. They have an automobile worth approximately $12,000 which is financed with a loan with a $7,000 balance. The family has furniture and other personal belongings on which has been placed an estimated liquidation value of $10,000.

Retirement assets consist solely of a vested pension benefit of $5,000. Employee A is entitled to this amount whenever he leaves his employment. This asset will continue to grow throughout his employment.

Investment assets include bank savings accounts (over and above the $22,000 designated for current needs) and some common stocks, $1,000 of which are in Individual Retirement Accounts. As you can see, they total $36,000.

At this point, we have simply prepared a financial statement for Worker A. Just how the investment assets should be invested cannot be answered without a more extensive risk evaluation of the family which will be done in the next chapter. Meanwhile, let's go through the process of looking at the financial statements of Manager B and Executive C to help become more familiar with just how personal financial statements are constructed.

Table II is the financial picture of Manager B. You might recall that he has a salary of $100,000, is 55 years old, and has a non-working spouse and adult children. The couple has a net worth of $635,000 split about evenly between equity in a home, various retirement assets, and a variety of investments.

In the current section, the couple has a loan outstanding of $3,000 and is planning an extensive vacation which will cost about $10,000. I have arbitrarily assigned $20,000 of savings to the current cash account to cover all current obligations and to provide a reserve of $7,000.

Permanent assets include a home worth an estimated $300,000 which has a mortgage of $140,000. They have automobiles worth about $18,000 and personal belongings with an estimated liquidation value of $15,000.

Manager B has a retirement plan with his employer and has a vested benefit of $125,000 which he is entitled to whenever he leaves the company and which will continue to grow as long as he continues to work. Manager B also has $50,000 in a company savings plan against which he has a loan of $25,000 which was used to finance automobile and other purchases. Manager B also has $45,000 in deferred compensation accounts with his employer.

The family has $250,000 of investments in stocks, bonds, bank accounts and other cash equivalents. Again, we will take a more detailed look at Manager B's investments later.

TABLE II
MANAGER B BALANCE SHEET

CURRENT	ASSETS	LIABILITIES	NET WORTH
Cash	$20,000	$0	$20,000
Accts Receivable	0	0	0
Amounts Owed	0	3,000	(3,000)
Anticipated Liabilities	0	10,000	(10,000)
Other	0	0	0
	20,000	13,000	7,000
PERMANENT			
Home & Mortgage	300,000	140,000	160,000
Autos & Auto Loans	18,000	0	18,000
Business Interests	0	0	0
Other	15,000	0	15,000
	333,000	140,000	193,000
RETIREMENT			
Vested Pension	125,000	0	125,000
IRA/Keough Accounts	0	0	0
Savings/401K Plan	50,000	25,000	25,000
Deferred Compensation	45,000	0	45,000
Other	0	0	0
	220,000	25,000	195,000
INVESTMENT			
Cash Reserve	95,000	0	95,000
Bonds	70,000	0	70,000
Stocks	85,000	10,000	75,000
Real Estate	0	0	0
Other	0	0	0
	250,000	10,000	240,000
TOTALS	$823,000	$188,000	**$635,000**

TABLE III
EXECUTIVE C BALANCE SHEET

CURRENT	ASSETS	LIABILITIES	NET WORTH
Cash	$30,000	$0	$30,000
Accts Receivable	10,000	0	10,000
Amounts Owed	0	20,000	(20,000)
Anticipated Liabilities	0	0	0
Other	0	0	0
	40,000	20,000	20,000
PERMANENT			
Home & Mortgage	400,000	175,000	225,000
Autos & Auto Loans	50,000	0	50,000
Business Interests	900,000	0	900,000
Other	40,000	0	40,000
	1,390,000	175,000	1,215,000
RETIREMENT			
Vested Pension	0	0	0
IRA/Keough Accounts	0	0	0
Savings/401K Plan	0	0	0
Deferred Compensation	40,000	0	40,000
Other	0	0	0
	40,000	0	40,000
INVESTMENT			
Cash Reserve	10,000	0	10,000
Bonds	0	0	0
Stocks	900,000	100,000	800,000
Real Estate	200,000	50,000	150,000
Other	10,000	0	10,000
	1,120,000	150,000	970,000
TOTALS	$2,590,000	$345,000	**$2,245,000**

The balance sheet of Executive C is reflected in Table III. She earns $500,000 per year in a self-owned business, is 40 years old, and has a spouse who is also a high earner. This couple has substantial net worth.

Executive C has been assigned $30,000 of current cash to cover a $20,000 extraordinary obligation and to provide a modest reserve. Annual income is more than sufficient to cover normal living expenses and to add to savings.

The couple has permanent assets consisting of a mortgaged home, automobiles, and $40,000 of jewelry and other personal assets. In addition, they own a business with a net worth of $900,000. I believe this is the appropriate place to reflect the business since it does not fall into the category of discretionary investment.

The couple has no pension but has $200,000 in a tax deferred Keough retirement account. These accounts are in the investment section of the balance sheet. They also have $40,000 in deferred compensation.

Investments of $1,120,000 are mainly in stocks and a vacation home. There are margin account borrowings against the stock and a mortgage on the vacation home. Again, in later chapters we will discuss the nature and propriety of Executive C's investments.

CONCLUSIONS

This chapter's message is simple: you cannot be in total control of your investment process if you haven't identified the extent of your assets available for discretionary investing. And you probably cannot know the extent of your investible assets without going through some type of self accounting process such as has been described in the examples in this chapter.

Bear in mind that the format reflects my preference but certainly is not the only possible one to use in constructing a personal balance sheet. Those familiar with business balance sheets may find that format more acceptable. And there are undoubtedly many possible variations of each. I believe the critical needs , regardless of format, are to identify current assets and liabilities, investible assets, and a reasonable approximation of net worth.

A most important point to understand is that exactness is not critical for this process. The end product is a guide for use in managing your affairs, not a financial statement that is subject to audit scrutiny. If any given asset or liability proves to be incorrect by 5% or 10%, it is not a case for concern. If Manager B's net worth is really $600,000 rather than $635,000, there is not reason for concern nor will the investment process be any different.

The precise value of some items may be difficult or even impossible to determine. For example, the market value of your home cannot really be known until you actually sell it. The same holds true for the value of automobiles, vacation homes, personal effects, etc.

Your vested pension benefit may be the most difficult asset to value. If it cannot be realistically estimated, perhaps with a phone call to your pension administrator, it may make sense to eliminate it from your balance sheet. But a reasonable estimate is worth the attempt because the figure can be quite large and therefore important to your overall invest-ment risk evaluation.

A final point relative to your personal balance sheet is that it needs to be treated as a dynamic document. Values change from time to time and it is important to update on a regular basis. A good time might well be as you wrestle with the process of getting your personal income tax returns filed.

CHAPTER V

Measure Your Risk Tolerance

CHAPTER V

MEASURE YOUR RISK TOLERANCE

If calculating your investible assets is the first thing you should address in the investment process, measuring your risk tolerance is the most important. It also completes the internal phase of the investment process and concludes by telling you how much risk you can absorb, setting the stage for determining how your investments should be allocated among the various investment choices.

What do we mean by risk tolerance? Simply put, it is your ability, based on several critical factors, to survive temporary declines in the value of your investible assets without significantly impairing your financial health. The key word is "temporary". Under no circumstances do I advocate that the average individual investor get involved with any investments which might result in a "permanent" decline in value.

This process has the same purpose as a professional investor determining whether his endowment fund is sufficiently funded to allow investing in higher risk, but higher likely return assets, or whether the fund should be managed more conservatively.

I believe there are five critical factors which need consideration in measuring your tolerance for investment risk. I have labeled these factors Life Stage, Cash Flow, Income Expectation, Financial Size, and Financial Quality. In my view, all are of significant and approximately equal in importance.

LIFE STAGE

Life stage is the factor we will begin with. It is an attempt to portray your particular situation from the standpoint of the various life stages most of us travel through. It is a process of categorizing all of us into one of five groups: Startup, Accumulation, Consumption, Development, and Harvest. It is, of course, an oversimplification and therefore the process allows for the use of judgement in it's application.

Startup is the risk category I assign to people usually in the very early stage of their adult lives. It generally fits those under 30 years of age, either single or married, with or without children. This group has significant years to accumulate assets and plenty of time to rebound from financial adversity and therefore I consider this category very low risk and therefore able to tolerate significant risk. Unfortunately, however, this group frequently has few assets which, as we will see later, may result in a very high overall risk assessment.

Accumulation is the next lowest investment risk group. People in this group are generally in the 50-60 age bracket. They have their major heavy expenditures behind them (home, education of children, etc.) and are enjoying their years of greatest earning power and disposable income and are saving for retirement. They have a considerable number of income producing years ahead of them. These factors indicate a risk profile which should allow these folks to absorb considerable risk.

Consumption is the middle life stage category group. People in this group are frequently in the 40-50 age bracket and in the midst of their heaviest life expenditures. However, they have considerable productive years ahead of them and, to the extent extra assets are available, they can absorb significant investment risk. Unfortunately, many in this group do not have assets available for discretionary investing and probably won't until their children are off on their own.

Development is the next highest risk category. Those in this group are generally 30-40 years old and are in or very close to their high expenditure period (children's education, home purchase or upgrade etc.). Because most assets will probably be needed for all or a major portion of these expenditures, it is not prudent to have most assets invested in things which may be subject to temporary declines in value. This is a time when liquidity is usually of extreme importance.

Harvest is the highest risk life stage category and is generally reserved for those over 60 years old, who are at or near retirement, and who will need their invested assets for normal living expenses. This is time when investment risk must be minimized for their may not be income generating opportunity available to recover from poor investment results.

The five life stage categories cannot be applied rigidly. For example, a 35 year old single person with no near term likelihood for major extraordinary expenses, is more appropriately in the Startup category (very low risk profile) rather than in the development category which I suggested as appropriate for a 35 year old. A 55 year old couple with young children yet to be educated are more appropriately categorized in the development group since they may be unable to tolerate significant risk at this time.

CASH FLOW

Cash flow is the next critical factor we will discuss in assessing ability to handle investment risk. I measure cash flow based on residual cash flow after all required expenditures have been made. I do not give cash flow from investments full value since that is really the result we are trying to solve for.

If cash inflow is such that considerable cash is left after all household expenditures and contingencies, this person has low cash flow risk. Conversely, if income is insufficient to fund household expenses and savings or investments must be continually liquidated, this is a high risk cash flow situation. We'll talk about how to apply the cash flow factor shortly.

INCOME EXPECTATIONS

Income is not worth much if it is not likely to continue. Therefore, it is important to factor income continuation prospects into your risk profile. Again, judgement is required , but who is better equipped to make this judgement than you. The important question that needs answering is whether your job or other income source is likely to continue. I put the question on a scale ranging from guaranteed (the lowest risk category) to unlikely (the highest risk category).

FINANCIAL SIZE

Financial size is another critical factor in the risk evaluation process. This is simply the determination of whether you have resources of sufficient magnitude to be able to absorb investment risk. In Chapter IV, Worker A's assets of $36,000 may not be sufficiently large to rate anything but a very high risk categorization. On the other hand, Executive C has $970,000 in investible net worth which probably represents a very low risk position. Again, we'll talk about application of the financial factor shortly.

FINANCIAL QUALITY

Financial quality is the final factor that I believe needs consideration in assessing one's ability to absorb risk. If a business has $1 billion in assets and an equal amount in liabilities, it has a very high risk balance sheet. Despite the company's significant size, the liabilities make it a poor risk and investment markets would demand very high interest rates, The same is true for the individual. Your financial quality must consider the extent of your liabilities, not just your assets, in determining just how much risk you should take on.

APPLICATION

Now that I've identified the five critical factors in measuring your tolerance for investment risk, the obvious question is how to apply these to each of us. My solution is to assign a value of one to five for each factor.

TABLE I
INVESTMENT RISK FACTORS

CATEGORY	RISK SCORE
LIFE STAGE	
Startup	1
Accumulation	2
Consumption	3
Development	4
Harvest	5
CASH FLOW (exclude investment income)	
20%+ more than needed	1
10%-20% more than needed	2
About neutral	3
10%-20% less than needed	4
20%+ less than needed	5
INCOME CONTINUATION (exclude investment income)	
Guaranteed	1
Highly likely	2
Probable	3
Questionable	4
Doubtful	5
FINANCIAL SIZE	
Investable assets over 4 times income	1
Investable assets 3-4 times income	2
Investable assets 2-3 times income	3
Investable assets 1-2 times income	4
Investable assets equal or less than income	5
FINANCIAL QUALITY	
Assets 5+ times liabilities	1
Assets 3-4 times liabilities	2
Assets 2-3 times liabilities	3
Assets 1-2 times liabilities	4
Assets equal or less than liabilities	5

Table I is a portrayal of the five critical risk factors and the application of each. As was stated before, each factor is given equal importance.

To calculate your overall risk profile, you must determine your position in each of the risk goupings. If your risk score is 1 in each category, your total risk score would be a very low 5. If your overall score is 5 in each category, your total score would be a very high 25. While the range goes from 5 to 25, most individuals will not likely score at either extreme, but it is a possibility.

But we're getting ahead of ourselves. You have calculated your risk score but so what! What the score means in terms of how much risk can be handled still hasn't been answered. Before we get into the details of trying to answer this key question, let's convert Table I into a chart which may give a better perspective.

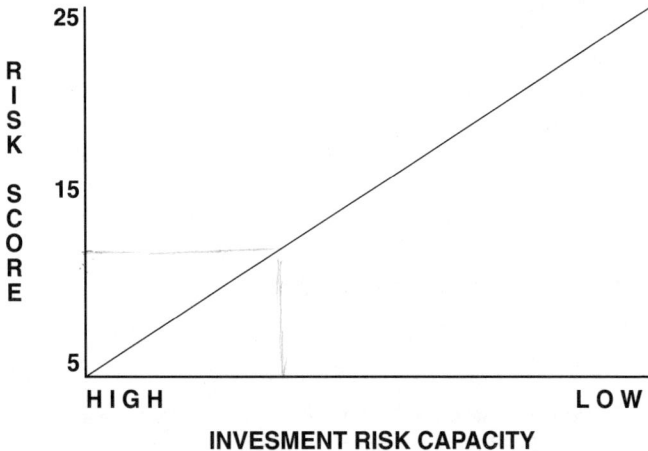

INVESMENT RISK CAPACITY

This chart is read by finding your total risk score on the vertical axis and locating this position on the diagonal line. If your risk score is 5, you have the highest capacity for investment risk. If your score is 12, as in the example, you are in the medium position. If your score is 25, you are in the highest risk position and can tolerate no risk.

Does this exercise really add value to the process of helping you invest like professionals? Unless you have developed your own evaluation process, or have such a strong financial position that you feel a process is unnecessary, I believe you should seriously consider it's merits. A structured method of evaluating your investment risk situation cannot hurt and may very well prevent you from some foolish investment decisions.

Let's next spend some time putting Employee A, Manager B, and through the risk measurement process.

EMPLOYEE A	RISK SCORE
Life Stage (37 years old, tuition needs)	4
Cash Flow (about neutral)	3
Income Expectations (no better than probable)	3
Financial Size (net worth 2+ times income)	4
Financial Quality (asset <2 times liabilities)	4
Score	18

Worker A has a fairly high risk score of 18, placing him in a position of not being able to tolerate much risk. Worker A is in a life stage with considerable extraordinary expenses ahead of him. The family's net worth is quite small, not providing much cushion in the event employment terminates. Also, cash flow is only neutral, indicating an unlikely ability to add to net worth in the foreseeable future.

We will use this risk score in Chapter VI when we will merge personal risk and investment risk to arrive at a conclusion as to how to allocate investible assets among the available choices.

MANAGER B	RISK SCORE
Life Stage (age 55, heavy expenses behind)	2
Cash Flow (about neutral)	3
Income Expectations (questionable)	4
Financial Size (net worth 4+ times income)	1
Financial Quality (assets 2+ times liabilities)	2
Score	12

Manager B has a medium risk score of 12 meaning some, but not significant risk can be tolerated. Despite a salary of $100,000, the couple has considerable debt in the form of a large mortgage and a loan against the employer's company savings plan. Manager B's likelihood of continued employment is questionable because of the company's poor earnings performance.

Manager B is approaching retirement and it is a good time to raise the issue of how to measure "financial size" for retirees. The "financial size" risk factor is a multiple of income. Since income changes dramatically upon retirement, the formula needs to be revised for retirees. I believe the following formula is an appropriate substitute:

	RISK SCORE
Net worth 10+ times annual needs	1
Net worth 9-10 times annual needs	2
Net worth 7-8 times annual needs	3
Net worth 5-6 times annual needs	4
Net worth <5 times annual needs	5

EXECUTIVE C	RISK SCORE
Life Stage (age 40, heavy expenses ahead)	3
Cash Flow (significantly positive)	1
Income Expectations (highly likely)	2
Financial Size (4+ times income)	1
Financial Quality (assets 7+ times liabilities)	1
Score	8

Executive C has a very low risk score of 8, indicating a capacity to absorb significant investment risk. While there are high college tuition expenses on the horizon, the couple has adequate assets at this time to more than compensate.

While the evaluation process used by professionals to evaluate the riskiness of a retirement or endowment fund is different than this process, it's objectives are the same. If a retirement fund needs to have near term liquidity to meet pension payments, it is in a higher risk position than if no significant payments were required for many years. If a scholarship fund plans on distributing a significant portion of it's assets in the near term, it needs to be much more liquid than it would be if there were no plans to ever distribute fund principal.

This chapter completes our discussion of the internal steps in the investment process. The first step was determining the extent of assets available for investing as well as calculating total net worth. The second step has been to develop a risk profile. The combination of the two can now be used in conjunction with appropriate external factors covered in earlier chapters to complete the investment process.

CHAPTER VI

Allocating Your Investible Assets

CHAPTER VI

ALLOCATING YOUR INVESTIBLE ASSETS

If measuring your tolerance to absorb investment risk is the most important step in the personal investment process, allocating your investible assets among the available investment choices is a close second. In previous chapters, we have covered three important steps leading to the asset allocation decision:

- measurement of your individual tolerance for investment risk. Recall that we defined investment risk as the potential for temporary or permanent decline in the market value of your investments.

- identification of the elements which cause permanent or temporary declines in investment values; market movements from economic or political forces; the inability to convert an investment to cash (liquidity risk); foreign currency risk; market or security volatility; and credit or business risk.

- expectations for return on your investments based on 6+ decades of market history.

This chapter will deal with combining the three issues to allow you to determine how your investible assets should be allocated among the available investment options.

INDIVIDUAL RISK TOLERANCE

Lets begin by summarizing Table 1 in Chapter V, which is the attempt to quantify the key individual risk factors into a combined risk score which can range from 5 to 25.

Life Stage - ranging from a score of one for those in the startup phase of their lives and able to absorb significant risk, to five for those in the harvest period in which investments are needed for every day living expenses and risk must be minimized.

Cash Flow - ranging from a score of one for those with annual cash inflow more than 20% greater than needed, to five for those with cash inflow 20% less than needed and who therefore must rely heavily on investments for every day living expenses

Income Expectations - ranging from one for those whose future income is guaranteed, to five for those whose expectation for continued income is doubtful.

Financial Size - ranging from a score of one when investable assets are substantially greater than annual income, to a score of five when these assets are about equal to or less than income.

Financial Quality - ranging from a score of one when an individual's balance is very strong and assets are more than five times the size of liabilities, to a score of five when assets are about equal to or less than liabilities.

INVESTMENT RISK

It's also worth repeating the chart from Chapter III which, as we concluded, approximates the risk for each of the investment categories which are appropriate for most individuals:

-----------------RISK-----------------

	MARKET	CREDIT	LIQUIDITY	CURRENCY	VOLATILITY
CASH EQUIV.	LOW	LOW	LOW	NONE	NONE
U.S. BONDS	LOW	LOW	LOW	NONE	MODERATE
U.S. STOCKS	LOW	LOW	LOW	NONE	HIGH
FOR, STOCKS	LOW	LOW	LOW	HIGH	HIGH
REAL ESTATE	LOW	LOW	HIGH	NONE	MODERATE

We concluded that market risk is low because all of the above investment classes have a history of providing returns at least equal to inflation over the long run.

We said that credit risk exists for all investment categories but that we could minimize it simply through the process of broad diversification.

We concluded that real estate is the only investment category for which liquidity is a concern, assuming that major liquid investment markets and actively traded securities are used for all other investments

By eliminating all foreign investment classes from our world of investments worthy of risk, we are left only with foreign stocks with currency risk.

Volatility is a risk which is pervasive in all but the short term cash equivalent categories. While all other investment risks can be avoided, volatility risk cannot be avoided and must be managed through prudent asset allocation. We will discuss how to best deal with this risk later on.

INVESTMENT RETURN

In Chapter II we detailed the historical investment returns for the three asset classes which are appropriate for most individuals: U.S. Stocks, U.S. Bonds, and U.S. Cash Equivalents. This performance history is summarized as follows in "real" terms, that is, after deducting for inflation:

REAL INVESTMENT RETURN

	EQUITIES	BONDS	CASH
1930's	6.6%	5.4%	1.8%
1940's	4.0%	-3.4%	5.7%
1950's	18.2%	0.8%	0.6%
1960's	6.0%	2.4%	1.3%
1970's	0.4%	1.3%	0.9%
1980's	13.0%	6.6%	3.9%
60 YEARS	8.1%	2.2%	0.1%

MERGING INDIVIDUAL RISK , INVESTMENT RISK , AND INVESTMENT RETURN

We now need to merge the conclusions of Chapters II, III, and IV to answer the critical question of how your assets should be allocated among the stock, bond, and cash equivalent categories.

Before we begin there is one very important point to understand. There is no scientific or mathematical formula to give the perfect answer to this question. Many investment professionals spend their lives trying to find the answer. Most have only limited success and most have related it only to the investment process of institutions whose assets comprise most of the several trillion dollars comprising the securities markets.

Recognizing that this process has considerable "art" as well as "science" to it, this book has been written to help individuals find a process for conservative investing while, at the same time, allowing them to achieve results equal to the best professional investors.

The objective from this point is quite simple. It is the merger of the individual profile matrix with the investment risk matrix, influenced by the expected returns from the investment markets which are considered prudent for most investors.

Let's look at the individual and investment matrix summaries side by side.

INDIVIDUAL RISK   INVESTMENT RISK

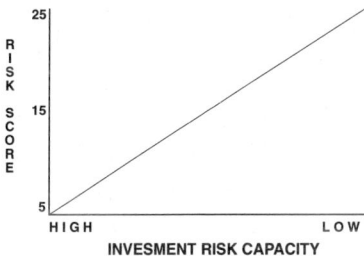

ASSET CLASS	VOLATILITY
CASH EQUIV.	NONE
U.S. BONDS	MODERATE
U.S. STOCKS	HIGH
FOREIGN STOCKS	HIGH
REAL ESTATE	MODERATE

Y-axis: RISK SCORE (5, 15, 25)
X-axis: INVESMENT RISK CAPACITY (HIGH ... LOW)

The individual risk chart plots the risk score range of 5-25 on the vertical axis and risk capacity on the horizontal axis. A score of 5 can tolerate significant risk; a score of 25 can tolerate no risk.

I have eliminated all of the investment risk categories except volatility. Why? Because the other risk factors are the same for all asset classes, there is no risk differentiation between them. The two exceptions are real estate liquidity risk and foreign stocks currency risk. As we concluded previously, these classes should not be used as a primary investment vehicle for individuals, but as a modest supplement at most.

The final step now is to merge the individual and investment risk summaries into one. The result is an asset allocation table such as the following:

ASSET CLASS	RISK SCORE				
	<8	8-12	13-17	18-22	22+
U.S. Stocks	75%	60%	40%	20%	0%
U.S. Bonds	15%	20%	20%	20%	20%
Cash	10%	20%	40%	60%	80%

This is not intended to be a rigid formula. It is intended as a guideline to sensibly approach your allocation of investible assets, rather than relying on pure instinct or advice from those without credentials or who might not be in a position to understand your particular circumstances.

The chart should be read as the upper limit of your investment position. If your risk score is 7, I believe you can tolerate as much as 75% of your assets in stocks. However, if you are uncomfortable with that high a stock allocation, don't hesitate to hold less in stocks and more in bonds or cash. If your risk score is 15, you may only be comfortable with 30% in stocks rather than 40% as called for above. Don't hesitate to reduce your stock allocation to 30% and add to either bonds or cash or both. You may also feel more comfortable arbitrarily moving yourself to a higher risk category (ie. giving yourself a higher risk score). Again, the point is to use the chart as your upper limit.

Because of the volatility of the stock market, I personally don't recommend that individuals hold more than 75% in stocks. Some in a very low risk position and with considerable knowledge of and comfort with equity investing might choose to exceed this limit.

The chart omits foreign stocks and real estate. It would be appropriate for those with risk scores less than 13 to put some of the U.S. stock allocation into foreign stocks. It also would be appropriate to put some bond allocation into real estate. Regardless of risk score, I do not recommend more than 10% of total assets in either category.

Let's now project the long term returns which should be expected from these allocations. This is done by using the 6+ decades real returns discussed previously. A 5% rate is assumed for both inflation and the expected return on cash investments.

ASSET CLASS	————————RISK SCORE————————				
	<8	8-12	13-17	18-22	22+
U.S. Stocks	9.8%	7.9%	5.2%	2.6%	0.0%
U.S. Bonds	1.1%	1.4%	1.4%	1.4%	1.4%
Cash	0.5%	1.0%	2.0%	3.0%	4.0%
Total Return	11.4%	10.3%	8.6%	7.0%	5.4%

The projected returns were calculated by applying the percent of investments in each category to the projected investment returns for each asset category.

For example, if your risk score is 14, 40% of your investments are recommended in stocks. Stocks provide a real return of 8.1% plus the assumed 5% inflation rate. 40% times 13.1% (8.1% real return plus 5% inflation) is 5.2%. The bond allocation is recommended at 20%. Bonds provide a 2.2% real return plus 5% inflation. 20% times 7.2% (2.2% real return plus 5% inflation) is 1.4%. The 40% cash allocation provides a 5% inflation return only. (40% times 5% return is 2.0%.)

The chart clearly demonstrates that the higher volatility risk you take the higher the return you should expect. But the key caveat is that, unless you can withstand market volatility, you could find your assets significantly depleted just when you need them. Without this volatility concern, the argument could be made that it would be foolish to invest in anything other than stocks.

Are the returns less than you expected? If so, I'm not surprised. But you can't argue with history. I believe it is very difficult to argue that there are ways to achieve higher returns if, in fact, history tells us that these are the long term U.S. capital market returns, or unless you can identify other investment categories that generate higher returns. If you can, you will achieve something that has not been achieved by the thousands of professionals who continually search for them.

This leads directly into the one remaining issue, namely, how should this investment allocation strategy be implemented. That is, which stocks, bonds, and cash equivalents should be used. The next chapter will be devoted to this issue.

Let's conclude with the question of how institutional funds have their assets allocated among the available investment choices.

Wells Fargo Investment Advisors suggests that it's institutional investors use an asset allocation of 48% stocks, 45% bonds, and 7% cash equivalents.*

Goldman Sachs indicates that private pension funds have 59.2% of their assets in equities and that public pension funds have 42.7% in equities.**

Pensions & Investments Age disclosed the following asset allocation survey of U.S. corporate defined benefit pension plans for 1990: Stocks, 48.7%, Bonds, 36.9%, Real Estate, 5.6%, Cash Equivalents, 7.5%, and Other, 1.3%.***

---

*INTRODUCING SIGMA, December 1990, Global Currencies, Wells Fargo Nikko Investment Advisors

**EQUITIES SUPPLY AND DEMAND, Goldman Sachs, October, 1990

***PENSIONS & INVESTMENTS AGE, January 21, 1991

The above, plus my own personal experiences with institutional funds and investment issues over the years lead me to conclude that U.S. pension and endowment funds typically have 40-50% of their assets invested in domestic stocks and about 5% in cash equivalents. That leaves the remaining 45-55% spread among bonds, real estate, foreign stocks, and perhaps a very small amount in other types of investments.

Certainly there is a wide dispersion among the public and private funds. I personally managed pension funds that allowed up to 85% of investments in equities. At the other extreme, I know of one reasonably large pension fund which only invests in government bonds. Many public funds continue to be quite conservative in their willingness to take on any kind of risk.

In my judgement, the facts don't support being overly conservative if a fund does not have the need to liquidate it's holdings in the near term. I don't understand the willingness to accept an approximate 2.2% bond market return for the sake of avoiding the volatility of stocks, as long as stocks won't have to be liquidated during market down cycles. I believe that those unwilling to take on significant stock market risk are confusing volatility risk and credit risk. As we have discussed, credit risk can be avoided with proper diversification.

CHAPTER VII

Selecting Your Investments

CHAPTER VII

SELECTING YOUR INVESTMENTS

We have covered a lot of ground in the first six chapters of this book. The objectives so far have been to get you positioned to invest. If the messages have been followed, you have determined the extent of your investible assets, measured your tolerance for investment risk, and used the results to allocate your investable assets among prudent investment choices. The remaining major issue is how to implement your allocation into actual investments.

Should you try to make your own specific investment decisions such as buying individual stocks and bonds? Should you utilize mutual funds, thereby allowing professionals to do the investment selection for you? Should you invest in specific real estate properties or buy into real estate pools managed by professionals? Should you use market index funds which allow you to equal but not exceed market returns without risking selecting the wrong investments or investment managers? Should you use a combination of these and other options in structuring your portfolio?

HOW SUCCESSFUL ARE THE PROFESSIONALS?

Since many of the choices involve the use of professionals, lets revisit the important question of just how successful they are. Recall my definition of "professional investor" in Chapter I as either those who manage funds belonging to institutions, individuals or businesses (investment managers), or those who direct the placement of funds with investment managers and are responsible for the results (fund sponsors). Also, recall my requirement for an independently verified record of investment performance to validate the professional's credentials.

Naturally, my own experiences prompted the writing of this book. Nowhere is this more pertinent than in dealing with the issue of whether professional investors are successful investors.

Under my definition of professional investor, I was one. I directed the investment of about $500 million of assets, about $350 million of which were pension funds belonging to workers in four countries, for a major U.S. corporation. I was responsible for the investment results. Those results were measured by an independent consultant and reported to the company and it's board of directors each quarter.

Was I a successful professional? You be the judge. While my responsibilities covered the late 1970's through the early 1990's, for sake of simplicity, let me focus on investment of United States pension funds for the full decade of the 1980's.

During the 1980's, the pension funds increased by 150% which was after investment performance as well as all expenses, contributions to the fund, and pension payments to retirees. The investment return was a compounded average of 15% per year, before investment manager fees. The fund was always conservatively managed and was well diversified between U.S. and foreign equities, bonds, real estate, and cash equivalents. The 15% compound return was the single most significant factor in the company's required annual pension contribution declining from about $13 million in the early 1980's to virtually nothing at the end of the decade. On the surface, this sounds like a very successful investment picture, but was it?

The benchmark against which the fund was measured was a weighted average of the index categories reflected in the fund; the U.S. stock portion was measured against the S&P 500 stock index, the bond portion against an appropriate Shearson-Lehman bond index, and so on. Our objective was to exceed the weighted average benchmark return after all investment manager fees.

During the 10 year period, the weighted average benchmark was about 16%, compared to the 15% we achieved. After factoring in management fees, our 15% trailed the benchmark by about 1.5% per year. Not the success that the 15% first appeared to be. But interestingly, our results were quite good compared to the results of other pension funds during this period.

This lack of totally satisfactory success occurred despite having a very prestigious consulting firm assist us during the entire period. It occurred despite constant attention from company management and it's board of directors. And most important, it occurred despite having some of the most prestigious investment management firms doing the actual investing - names like Alliance Capital, BEA Associates, Batterymarch Financial Management, Wells Fargo Investment Management, and a number of other lesser known but equally talented managers.

How could all this talent not even achieve a return equal to the market averages over this relatively long time frame? And does the same fact pattern exist for the professional investment world in general?

I believe that most professional investors underperform market averages over the long term (5-10 years). I offer the following arguments to support this conclusion:

ARGUMENT #1 - In Chapter I we discussed a study of Wyatt Asset Services Inc. The study is worth reviewing again.

Performance of 410 large institutional equity funds was analyzed for the decade 1980-89. Two 5 year periods, 1980-84 and 1985-89 were evaluated separately. The 410 fund universe included essentially all public equity-only mutual funds and many pooled equity funds of banks and insurance companies. Truly, the cream of professional money managers.

This study revealed the following results against the S&P 500 stock index benchmark:

1980-84
- 83 or 20% exceeded the S&P by more than 20%
- 39 or 10% exceeded the S&P by 10-20%
- 82 or 20% approximated the S&P
- 206 achieved less than 95% of the S&P return
- 108 achieved less than 80% of the S&P return

1985-89
- 1 exceeded the S&P by greater than 20%
- 6 or 1% exceeded the S&P by 10-20%
- 54 or 13% approximated the S&P
- 248 achieved less than 95% of the S&P return
- 148 achieved less than 80% of the S&P return
- 61 or 155 dropped out of the universe

- the lower performing funds in 1980-84 generally
continued to do poorly - most of the top performers
in 1980-84 were substandard performers in 1985-
89

The conclusion seems to be that , while some active equity
managers add value over market averages some of the time,
the large majority underperform over the longer term.

ARGUMENT #2 -In 1990, a *Wall Street Journal* article
focused on the investment recommendations of the ten
largest Wall Street brokerage firms whose performance was
studied from July 1,1986 to September 30,1990*. Over the
fifty-one month period, two firms easily outpaced the market
averages. The other seven firms trailed behind the market
averages and, as the article states, "often miserably behind". Again, the conclusion seems to be the same for the
major brokerage firms as it is for money managers - most
underperform market averages over the longer term.

ARGUMENT #3 - The Vanguard Group is a major manager of actively and passively managed equity and bond
mutual funds. In it's publication, "Some Plain Talk About
Investing", Vanguard reports that, for the 10 years ending
September 30, 1990, the S&P 500 index returned a cumulative 258.5% or 13.6% per year. During the same period,
average equity fund returned 185.0% or 11.0% per year.

Vanguard rightfully points out that most active equity
funds have cash reserves of at least 5-10% of assets. Conse-
quently, in a bull market period such as much of the 1980's,
indexes have had a natural advantage because they are
100% invested at all times.

*STREETS STOCK PICKERS STUMBLE IN QUARTER, Wall Street Journal,
November 13, 1990.

On the other hand, is it important to you "why" someone underperforms? Isn't the correct objective to outperform the market, especially if a manager is being paid a fee to do so, and not try to rationalize underperformance? Also, recall the 63 year performance statistics covered previously. In most years markets are up, which seems to suggest that, in most years, an index has this natural advantage. Or conversely, in most years, active managers have a disadvantage by being less than 100% invested.

ARGUMENT #4 - The July 7,1992 issue of the *Wall Street Journal* included an evaluation of the performance of the "biggest" mutual funds over periods up to 10 years through July 1992.

The 10 year winners were the Fidelity Magellan Fund managed, for the most part, by the now retired Peter Lynch, and Fidelity Select Health Fund. The average for all funds in this 10 year period was a cumulative 323%. The cumulative performance of the S&P 500 was 444%.

Again, strong evidence that even the largest managers (and therefore those considered very capable) cannot, as a group, exceed simple market averages.

ARGUMENT #5 - While some academics might disagree, many of us believe there is a correlation between interest rate movement and equity (as well as bond) price movement. Therefore, if an investor could find a reliable forecaster of interest rates, he or she would have a powerful tool to time market performance.

The October 20, 1989 issue of The Babson Staff Letter cited a 5-year interest rate forecasting study performed by

Merrill Lynch.* The study summarized the semi-annual interest rate forecasts of leading economists reported every January and July in the *Wall Street Journal*. Eleven 6-month forecasts were analyzed in terms of accuracy of interest rate movements over the next 6 months. Amazingly, the experts, as a group, were wrong 10 times out of 11. That is, interest rates moved in a different direction than the experts predicted.

ARGUMENT #6 - So far we've talked only about equity performance, but what about bonds? Charles Schwab & Co., a major brokerage firm, revealed some interesting mutual fund bond data in 1991.**

- 16 bond funds existed for at least 10 years. Not one of the 16 beat the 13.7% compound return of the Shearson-Lehman Corporate Bond Index for the prior 10 years (1981-90).

- 28 bond funds existed for at least 5 years. Not one of them beat the Shearson-Lehman Corporate Bond Index for the prior 5 years (1986-90).

- even more significant, none of the reported funds were able to exceed the performance of the Shearson-Lehman Government Bond Index for either the 5 or 10 year periods. I find this quite incredible considering that government bonds are guaranteed by the U.S. government and corporate bonds, of course, are not. Governments therefore carry a lower interest rate to compensate for the lower risk.

---

* INTEREST RATE FORECASTING, The Babson Staff Letter, October 20, 1989.
** MUTUAL FUND PERFORMANCE GUIDE, Fourth Quarter 1989, Charles Schwab & Co.

I believe that these arguments clearly demonstrate that most professional investors are not able to beat the average performance of the markets they are in, particularly after deducting transaction costs and management fees, which are generally in the range of 1%-2% of assets managed.

Is this conclusion possible, and, if so, why? There are many factors which impact the answer but those I feel are most relevant are as follows:

- professional investors "are" the market. They are sophisticated, intelligent, highly trained investors and all have access to the same information. Their ability to beat their equally capable peers becomes less and less probable as the group, as a whole, gets more and more capable. In other words, there are fewer and fewer market inefficiencies on which to capitalize.

- As we described earlier in the 63-year investment tables, most years are positive years for the investment markets. Since many, if not most professional managers have some cash on hand at all times, they are handicapped in their ability to equal or exceed market averages or indexes, which are always reflected as fully invested.

- Major world events which impact markets are not predictable and frequently happen very suddenly. As examples, the 1970's oil embargo, the 1980's junk bond fiasco, and the 1990's war with Iraq. Active management may be out of sync with these events while market averages reflect the full impact, both positive and negative, of all of them.

- Manager fees and transaction costs can further handicap active managers by as much as 2%.

DO AMATEURS BEAT THE PROFESSIONALS ?

This section will be very short because there is little available data on how well amateur or individual investors do in terms of investment success. Instinctively, it would seem that those who devote only a portion of their time to managing investments will not do as well as professionals who have substantial information and other resources at their fingertips and who devote all of their working lives to investing.

I also believe there is circumstantial evidence to suggest that amateurs don't perform as well. We know that, over time, equities are the best performing investment class. We also know that individuals have, on average, less than 20% of their assets in equities. I believe this strongly suggests that individuals have not had good equity investing results and therefore have elected to stay out of the equity (and probably bond) market and keep most of their assets in cash equivalents. By doing this, they have accepted returns that may equal, but do not exceed inflation. Not a good financial decision.

HOW DO WE SOLVE THE DILEMMA ?

Now that we've concluded that most amateur and professional investors cannot consistently beat market averages, where do we turn? If we approximate market averages, we can at least equal and probably exceed the returns generated by most professionals. But how do we get these average returns? Or should we be willing to accept less-than-market returns because that's as good as most experts are getting? Should we be satisfied as long as we achieve a "real" return -that is, a return on our investments which is above the inflation rate? My answer to these questions and I hope your answer is a resounding no!

There are ways to equal and possibly exceed market returns, and it can be accomplished with a minimum of effort, anguish, and risk. The answer falls into three simple investment strategies:

1)Limit equity investing to no-load (no commission) index mutual funds with low management fees and with demonstrated ability to approximate the index they are designed to match, or mutual funds of active equity or balanced managers who have long records of above market performance, after deducting all fees and expenses from the investment returns,

2)Limit bond investing to U.S. government bond or municipal mutual funds, but only those with managers having long records of above market performance, after deducting all fees and expenses from the investment returns.

3)Limit cash investments to U.S. government treasury bills, to deposits with banks (only to the limit of government insurance), or to high quality money market mutual funds with demonstrated records of good performance.

There is nothing magical about these rules. However, when they are applied in conjunction with your risk score, as determined in Chapter V, your results will be investment returns which are at least as good as most professional managers.

Let's review, in greater detail, the individual investment vehicles mentioned in the above rules.

EQUITY INDEX MUTUAL FUNDS: Equity index funds are designed to duplicate returns of specific indexes such as the S&P 500, or the returns of a specific block of companies based on size, such as the largest 1000 public companies. Managers accomplish this objective by either investing in every stock in their universe or, more typically, investing in a large sample of stocks which track the returns of the universe.

Index, or passive investing has become a popular vehicle for institutional investors.Billions are invested in this manner in the U.S. and the practice is spreading to other parts of the world. Some of the world's largest investment firms have very large index funds, including Banker's Trust Company, Mellon Capital, and State Street Bank and Trust Company, and Wells Fargo-Nikko Securities.

Why has indexing become so popular with institutions? For the same reasons we have been discussing. Active managers, on average, underperform market averages over time, after factoring in all fees and expenses. Index funds capture market returns, less fees and expenses which are typically very low.

Equity indexing can provide a safe, simple opportunity to achieve market returns. As we discussed, over time these returns are 11%-12%, or about 8% above inflation. What's more, these returns can be accomplished without worrying about trying to time the stock market, or fretting over what stocks you should be buying or selling, or whether your investment manager is doing the right job for you. And a particular benefit is the opportunity to have your performance report card available to you every day in most daily newspaper mutual fund listings.

I don't want to leave you with the impression that indexing is a new or revolutionary investment style. Pensions and Investment Age reported in July 1991 that the largest 50 or so index managers have $340 billion under management in equity and bond funds. This is a serious investment style and has been growing rapidly as more and more investment professionals deal with the difficulty of paying high fees for below market active investment results.

Has your broker or financial advisor recommended indexing? Probably not, because there are no commissions for them if you invest this way. You are able to invest yourself in no load (no commission) index funds by dealing directly with the mutual funds.

Are there any negatives to indexing? None that I can see as long as you don't have to sell in down markets. And if your have properly determined your risk profile and allocated your assets accordingly, you will have provided adequate emergency liquidity in other parts of your investment portfolio to carry you through market downturns.

The only negative I've heard discussed is that indexing takes the fun out of investing. How boring it must be to put money in an index fund and not have the opportunity to make your own buy and sell decisions. My answer is that I would rather get my recreation on the golf course or on the beach and not by trying to figure out securities markets. Why should I risk my life savings with amateur investing or with managers who are unlikely to achieve average market returns when I can simply and inexpensively achieve as good a return on my money by simply indexing.

We've pointed out that international equity investing may be an appropriate place for part of your investment dollars but, because of currency risk, probably should be limited to 5% or so of your total portfolio.

In fact, in the 1980's, a broad international index of equities outperformed the S&P 500 index by a wide margin, even after all affects of converting each respective foreign currency to U.S. dollars. Looking at individual countries shows a less appealing picture because of very significant volatility.

I feel the message is similar to the U.S. equity message - investing in a broad international equity index makes considerable sense. Investing in active international equity management or country funds adds risk that I don't feel is worth taking.

Many U.S. pension and endowment funds do not invest internationally, and those that do typically have less than 15% of their assets in this category. This suggests to me that a 5% limit is appropriate for the individual.

ACTIVE EQUITY MUTUAL FUNDS: Some active equity managers beat market averages over the long term, but not many. I've pointed out that, in any given year, about 50% will outperform before deducting management fees, and slightly less than 50% will outperform after fees. The real problem is the inability of most to outperform over a several year time frame. The problem for the investor is to try to figure out who the future outperformers will be.

Pension and Investments Age Evaluation Report (PIPER) reported that, for the decade of the 1980's, the average performance for 337 banks and insurance companies was 16.7% per year, compared to 17.6% for the S&P 500.* Almost 75% of managers underperformed over the full 10 year period.

Charles Schwab Mutual Funds Performance Guide lists the investment performance of a long list of mutual funds sold through the Schwab organization. The report shows that, for the 1980's, only 17 of 84 funds outperformed the S&P 500. And this statistic does not reflect the funds which existed at the beginning of the decade and not at the end. They were obviously not good performers and, if included, would result in an even greater percent of underperformers.

So again, the issue at hand is to identify those managers with good long term records and assume they will continue to outperform. I don't put a high degree of confidence in this exercise but I accept it as a way to invest with a reasonable probability of either beating market averages or coming close.

Who are these managers? The top equity manager for the decade of the 1980's was Peter Lynch manager of the Fidelity

PENSIONS & INVESTMENTS PERFORMANCE EVALUATION REPORT, December 31, 1990, Pensions & Investments, Rogers, Casey

Magellan Fund. but unfortunately Mr. Lynch has since retired from managing the fund. And there are others with good long-term records as of this writing such as Financial Industrial Income Fund, Janus Fund and IAI Regional Fund to name a few.

Is it smart to try to identify the few managers who might be the top performers in the next decade? Probably not as smart a sticking with index funds. But for those who need more excitement in their lives, investing with managers with excellent long term performance records is prudent.

There are hundreds of equity mutual funds to chose from and many ways of selecting individual funds. My selection criterion limits investing only to funds with the following characteristics:

- No-load (no commission) to buy or sell.

- long and medium term performance records above that of benchmark averages.

- The same manager as during the period in which the above benchmark performance was achieved.

- Broad diversification as opposed to sector, country, or other narrowly invested funds.

In conclusion, the recommended way to invest in pure equities is through the use of no load, low fee index funds which are designed to match the performance of specific indexes such as the S&P 500. A second, and less enthusiastically endorsed way is to invest in mutual funds with proven long term records of superior performance.

BALANCED FUNDS: Balanced funds are actively managed mutual funds which invest in a combination of stocks, bonds, and cash equivalents bases on their perception of which of the categories are the best short term value.

Balanced management was once the prevalent way to invest. It is a market timing process and grew out of favor in the 1970's as market timing was shown to be a difficult process with which to invest successfully. CGM Mutual and Vanguard Asset Allocation are balanced funds which have been successful, using the same criterion as described previously for judging active equity managers.

The Vanguard fund is a relatively new mutual fund and qualifies based on it's record as an institutional manager. It's investment process is described as tactical asset allocation (TAA). TAA, as in the Vanguard fund, was developed in the early 1970's by William L. Fouse, then of Wells Fargo Investment Management and later Mellon Capital. It is a process of using an accepted quantitative investment tool, the dividend discount model, to determine the relative investment value of the S&P 500, long term U.S. government bonds, and U.S. Treasury bills. The objective of TAA is to provide equity returns over the very long term without the short term volatility of equities. It has an excellent long term performance record.

This TAA process has generated excellent results and I recommend it as a supplement to pure stocks, bonds, an cash equivalent investments. TAA has been a label that others now use for other multiple asset investment styles. Some I'm sure are very good and others seem to be the old balanced management with a different wrapper. Caution should be exercised when selecting a TAA manager to be sure you know exactly what you are getting and, most important, what the long term investment results have been.

It's appropriate to spend one additional moment on balanced management. A *Wall Street Journal* article of August 13, 1991 carried a headline. "Balanced Mutual Funds Are Back In The Limelight". It referred to balanced mutual funds as one of the oldest and sleepiest areas of fund investing. The article also reported that the average balanced fund returned 51.5% for the past 5 years compared to 75.6% for the S&P 500 index. It sounds to me like this investment style is still sleeping.

ACTIVE BOND FUNDS: I see no strong reason to invest in bonds funds other than those limited to U.S. government bonds. There is no question that corporate bonds pay higher interest rates, but let me give you three reasons why I feel government bonds make more sense.

First, active bond managers seem unable to beat market averages over time, not unlike the results for equity managers. And, as we pointed out previously, most professional bond managers have been unsuccessful in even beating the performance of government bond averages despite the higher interest rates of corporates.

Second, government bonds return less than 1% less than corporate bonds (8/10's of 1% over the 60 years ending 1989). This means that for every $100,000 you have invested in bonds, your annual pretax return is only about $800 more with corporate bonds than with governments. And this assumes you have found an active bond manager who can outperform the market.

Third and perhaps more important, government bonds are guaranteed by the U.S. government. Corporate bonds carry the risk of default (although I recognize that this risk can be minimized with adequate diversification).

Municipal bond mutual funds are one exception to my position that bond investing should be limited to U.S. government bond funds only. Municipal funds have significant tax benefit in that the interest they pay is tax free. Investors should compare the expected yields of U.S government mutual funds and very high quality municipal funds, and if municipals look more attractive, consider using a portion for their portfolios.

CASH EQUIVALENTS: Your cash equivalents are there to meet liquidity and emergency needs and not to maximize return. The most important requirement is to have the assets when you need them. Just as it makes little sense for the individual to chase fractional return differences on bond investments, it makes even less sense to chase even smaller differentials in cash investments.

The answer to how your cash equivalent funds should be invested is simple - put the funds where there is either no risk or extremely low risk of loss. The "no risk" options are U.S. treasury bills and bank deposits fully guaranteed by the U.S. government. The "low risk" option is very well diversified, high quality money market funds.

FUN MONEY: One problem many of you will find with my investment process is that it takes all of the fun out of trying to beat the market. Won't it be boring to put everything in indexed or active mutual funds. How can I bypass the opportunity to invest in that "hot tip" that might be the next Intel or Walmart or Disney.

For those of you that need the therapeutic value of investing on your own, by all means take some of your assets and "do your thing". But do it only under the following rules. First, allocate no more than 5% of your assets for this "fun" investing. And second, keep track of your investment performance just as the other 95% of your investments are being measured. You may find you're the next Peter Lynch. More likely, you'll have a difficult time in achieving performance better than the rest of your investment portfolio and probably will find it much poorer.

TAX CONSIDERATIONS

This book is not intended to discuss income taxes in any detail, nor is the author a tax expert. Nevertheless, the basic tax considerations for individuals of owning each of the recommended investment vehicles needs some comment.

Individual government and corporate bonds pay interest, which is taxable to the holders when paid. In addition, if bonds are sold prior to maturity, at a gain or loss compared to the price paid for them, the gain or loss is subject to tax treatment.

Taxable bond mutual funds distribute interest to shareholders in the year received. In addition, if individual bonds within a fund are sold at gains or losses, these gains or losses are distributed to shareholders in the year realized. When shares in a bond mutual fund are sold, the difference between purchase price, adjusted for previously received taxable gains and losses, and the selling price is taxable.

Municipal bonds and municipal bond mutual funds have

the advantage of interest being non-taxable. This tax free status may apply to state and local income taxes as well as federal taxes, depending on the nature of the particular bonds. Because of this tax benefit, municipal bonds pay lower interest rates than equal quality taxable bonds. Gains and losses on the sale of municipal bonds and municipal bond mutual funds are subject to tax in the same manner as taxable bonds.

Individual equities (stocks) have a tax advantage over bonds. Investment return is a combination of dividends and appreciation (or depreciation). While dividends are taxable when paid, appreciation is taxable only when a stock is sold. The tax impact of appreciation or depreciation can, therefore, be deferred indefinitely. This tax benefit is particularly valuable because it can be timed to complement other considerations in a given tax year.

Equity mutual funds are taxed the same as individual equities, except that the individual does not have the ability to time all gains or losses. Dividends are taxable to shareholders in the year paid. Appreciation or depreciation on stocks sold is taxable when realized and distributed to shareholders. When fund shares are sold, as with taxable bond funds, the difference between cost and adjusted selling price is taxable in the year of sale.

Equity mutual funds with high turnover usually generate more current taxable income than funds with low turnover. A particular advantage with index mutual funds is low turnover and therefore usually low current taxes.

Real estate has the same tax deferral benefit as equities. Rental income (net of expenses) is taxable currently while gains and losses are deferred until sale. Real estate may also provide current depreciation deductions, which frequently is an important ownership factor to real estate investors.

Many investors focus on taxes as the principal investment issue. For example, many people will only invest in tax free municipals. By doing this, taxes are avoided but total portfolio return is frequently less than portfolios with an allocation to quality equities or equity funds. Other individuals may focus their investments in real estate to gain the early depreciation benefit, with tax on gains deferred until sale. Unfortunately, as many who bought real estate limited partnerships in the 1980's learned, many times these gains do not happen and the end result is a poor investment which may not even be saleable when the investor needs the cash.

I feel that the investor is better served to make the best long term investment choices and only use tax considerations as one of the many factors in the decision process.

CHAPTER VIII

Implement, Monitor, And Adjust

CHAPTER VIII
IMPLEMENT, MONITOR, AND ADJUST

IMPLEMENT

We have concluded how your investible assets should be allocated among the appropriate investment classes - stocks, bonds, cash equivalents, and possibly real estate. We have also concluded that the prudent vehicles to use to apply this allocation are index mutual funds, carefully selected actively managed mutual funds, and risk free or very low risk money market funds (or insured bank deposits if you prefer). The remaining issue is how this strategy should be implemented or, to put it another way, how your actual portfolio should be structured.

There is no single answer to portfolio structure. The most important rule is to continue the diversification philosophy that caused us to conclude that diversified index and active mutual funds were appropriate vehicles to minimize credit risk (risk that a single or small number of securities can move contrary to the market in which it exists). Applying this rule means that you should limit the percent of your portfolio with any active fund manager, and at least consider spreading your index fund and money market allocations over more than one investment.

Before you make your final decision on which funds you will use, be sure you have read fund prospectuses and any other information you can locate about each fund - it's history, it's investment philosophy, and most important, whether the style and investment manager are the same today as they were when the performance which attracted you was achieved.

The following tables describe some possible scenarios for each of the top four allocation categories. I have omitted detailing the highest risk (22+ risk score) because it can be summarized by simply stating that implementation can be accomplished by having at least 80% in safe cash equivalents and 20% in one or more government bond funds.

TABLE I
75% STOCKS/15% BONDS/10% CASH ALLOCATION

	TOTAL	STOCKS	BONDS	CASH
ALTERNATIVE #1				
Equity index funds	60%	60%		
Balanced funds	30%	15%	15%	
Risk free cash	10%			10%
	100%	75%	15%	10%
ALTERNATIVE #2				
Equity index funds	40%	40%		
Balanced funds	20%	10%	10%	
Active equity funds	25%	25%		
Active bond funds	5%		5%	
Risk free cash	10%			10%
	100%	75%	15%	10%
ALTERNATIVE #3				
Equity index funds	25%	25%		
Balanced funds	20%	10%	10%	
Active equity funds	40%	40%		
Active bond funds	5%		5%	
Risk free cash	10%			10%
	100%	75%	15%	10%

Invest Like The Successful Pros

TABLE II
60% STOCKS/20% BONDS/20% CASH ALLOCATION

	TOTAL	STOCKS	BONDS	CASH
ALTERNATIVE #1				
Equity index funds	45%	45%		
Balanced funds	30%	15%	15%	
Active bond funds	5%		5%	
Risk free cash	20%			20%
	100%	60%	20%	20%
ALTERNATIVE #2				
Equity index funds	30%	30%		
Balanced funds	20%	10%	10%	
Active equity funds	20%	20%		
Active bond funds	10%		10%	
Risk free cash	20%			20%
	100%	60%	20%	20%
ALTERNATIVE #3				
Equity index funds	20%	20%		
Balanced funds	20%	10%	10%	
Active equity funds	30%	30%		
Active bond funds	10%		10%	
Risk free cash	20%			20%
	100%	60%	20%	20%

TABLE III
40% STOCKS/20% BONDS/40% CASH ALLOCATION

	TOTAL	STOCKS	BONDS	CASH
ALTERNATIVE #1				
Equity index funds	25%	25%		
Balanced funds	30%	15%	15%	
Active bond funds	5%		5%	
Risk free cash	40%			40%
	100%	40%	20%	40%
ALTERNATIVE #2				
Equity index funds	20%	20%		
Balanced funds	20%	10%	10%	
Active equity funds	10%	10%		
Active bond funds	10%		10%	
Risk free cash	40%			40%
	100%	40%	20%	40%
ALTERNATIVE #3				
Equity index funds	15%	15%		
Balanced funds	26%	13%	13%	
Active equity funds	12%	12%		
Active bond funds	7%		7%	
Risk free cash	40%			40%
	100%	40%	20%	40%

TABLE IV
20% STOCKS/20% BONDS/60% CASH ALLOCATION

	TOTAL	STOCKS	BONDS	CASH
ALTERNATIVE #1				
Equity index funds	10%	10%		
Balanced funds	20%	10%	10%	
Active bond funds	10%		10%	
Risk free cash	60%			60%
	100%	20%	20%	60%
ALTERNATIVE #2				
Equity index funds	10%	10%		
Balanced funds	10%	5%	5%	
Active equity funds	5%	5%		
Active bond funds	15%		15%	
Risk free cash	60%			60%
	100%	20%	20%	60%
ALTERNATIVE #3				
Equity index funds	5%	5%		
Balanced funds	20%	10%	10%	
Active equity funds	5%	5%		
Active bond funds	10%	10%		
Risk free cash	60%			60%
	100%	20%	20%	60%

There are several rules which, I believe, should be implicit in your investment implementation for the sake of achieving the benefits of broad diversification. They are as follows:

- a significant portion of the equity allocation, under any allocation scenario, should be in equity index funds. I suggest at least 50% of your equity portfolio.

- limit an investment in a single index fund to 30% of your total portfolio.

- a single active (equity or bond) or balanced fund should be limited to 10% of your total portfolio. I see no reason to retain this limitation with the Vanguard Asset Allocation Fund because it essentially invests in index-type products, and suggest a 20% limitation.

A critical issue in the implementation process is timing. This is a long term investment strategy so timing is not a long term issue. But I believe it is a short term issue, particularly if you are making a major portfolio overhaul or if you are about to move a significant sum from one investment strategy or class to another.

The concern I have is the risk of making a major investment just before a significant market drop. The best example would have been a major move into the U.S. stock market just before the October 1987 market crash. While you would have eventually recovered your losses, you could have avoided the full effect of the crash by timing your investing.

The process would have been to spread your investment implementation over a several month or several quarter time frame. Lets assume you received a lump sum pension distribution in August 1987 and were putting most of it in equity investments. An immediate investment of the total would have resulted in a 22% loss in the fourth quarter, essentially all of which would have occurred in October. Had you decided to exercise caution and invest 10% per month over 10 months, the average cost of your investment portfolio would have been significantly less. The 22% loss would have been on only 20-30% of your portfolio rather than 100%.

The opposite scenario might, of course, occur with a quick market surge. But isn't it prudent to avoid risk of major loss compared to the opposite risk that your long term investment portfolio might have a higher cost basis. Recovering a 22% loss is a frightening prospect.

MONITOR

After you've gone to the trouble of developing and implementing an investment program, the worst thing you can do is put it totally on "automatic pilot" and stop paying attention to it. Even if your investments are structured in the most passive (indexed) way, you need to address the investment performance as well revisit your own personal financial situation from time to time.

Before you can effectively monitor investment performance, however, you need to have something to measure against. There is no single reported figure against which you can measure investment performance so it's necessary to create your own. The most appropriate way is to set an individual benchmark for each investment you make. As examples;

> - an investment in an S&P 500 index fund can be measured against the performance of the S&P

index which gets reported regularly in financial publications. Note that your index will probably slightly underperform the reported index which is free of transaction costs and management fees.

- an investment in other indexes such as the Schwab 1000 or Russell 2000 or Wilshire 5000 should be measured against the reported results of these indexes, again recognizing the transaction fee and management fee differences.

- bond fund investments should have as benchmarks one of the Shearson-Lehman bond indexes which are reported regularly in the financial press. The particular Shearson-Lehman index will depend on whether your bond fund is short, intermediate or long term in duration.

- Asset Allocation or balanced funds should be measured against a composite of stock and bond indexes. A simple 2-point average of the S&P 500 index and the Shearson-Lehman intermediate or long term bond index might be appropriate, but you should consider other options based on the stated objectives of your fund.

- your cash equivalent investments can be measured against the investment results of money market funds or US treasury bills or notes or other reportings in the financial press.

ADJUST

The process of monitoring your investment situation and investment performance should be done at least on an annual basis. Adjustment must be considered based on the following:

- Revisit your financial risk profile. Has your situation changed significantly? Are you now in a position to take on more investment volatility risk? Or are you perhaps in a higher risk category and should consider reducing your investment risk?

- Measure the performance of each of your investments to determine if they are doing exactly they are intended to do. If not, you should eliminate the investment and replace it with something else.

- Consider the need to rebalance your portfolio if the percentage you now have in one or more investment class or specific investment is different than when you allocated your assets.

This opens the critical issue of how long you should stay with an underperforming investment before you make a change. One bad quarter? One year? A market cycle, which can easily span five or six years?

There is no easy answer to this question. It is one of the most difficult issues that professionals are faced with. I feel the best way to deal with this issue is to establish rigid rules to govern when you should sell an investment and replace it with something else.

The rules or formula you use to monitor performance are those you are comfortable with. You might consider the following:

- Index funds are expected to achieve returns equal to their benchmarks, less transaction costs and management fees, both of which should be very low. You may want to set a formula that calls for selling a fund after two consecutive years of underperforming the benchmark by more than 1/2% or 3/4% each year.

- Active managers are expected to "beat the market" which is why you hired them. But we know that even the best manager can't beat the market every year. So you might consider set a rule to sell a fund if it has underperformed it's benchmark for three consecutive years by a cumulative total of more than five or ten percentage points.

- Balanced funds might have a sell formula based on failing to achieve their benchmark over the same time frame set for active managers, and with the same five or ten percentage point formula.

Part of the monitoring process is to periodically rebalance your portfolio back to it's original structure as the need occurs. Let's assume an asset allocation of 60% equities, 20% bonds, and 20% cash. If your equities have been returning significantly more than your bonds and cash investments, equities will eventually become more than 60% of your portfolio. At some point you need to get back to your original asset allocation objective.

I think it makes sense to make this evaluation once each year. It isn't necessary to rebalance if only minor changes are required such as adjustment of a few percent. But, for example, if your allocation has become 70% equities, 15% bonds, and 15% cash, it would be wise to rebalance your entire portfolio, This would be accomplished by selling some equities and using the proceeds to buy some bonds and cash equivalents to get yourself back to 60%, 20%, 20%.

Rebalancing is not an easy concept to accept. It frequently means that you must sell some of that which has performed very well for you. But you can't let emotions dictate. If your risk profile says you can tolerate 60% of your money in equities, you should be uncomfortable letting it stay at 70% for an extended time. It is still your most volatile investment group and no market stays on an upward trend line forever.

CHAPTER IX

The 10 Investment Sins Revisited

CHAPTER IX

THE 10 INVESTMENT SINS REVISITED

Way back in Chapter I we pointed out the 10 most significant investment "sins". They were as follows:

- having unrealistic expectations
- not establishing objectives
- not understanding risk
- not determining your investable assets
- accepting poor advice
- trying to time market moves
- not diversifying
- not cost averaging
- not monitoring results
- having no "sell" discipline

Let's review to see if we have discussed ways of managing your investments to avoid each of these "sins".

HAVING UNREALISTIC EXPECTATIONS: Chapter II was mainly devoted to reviewing investment choices and, most important, examining 63 years of historical investment returns.

The chapter clearly pointed out that equities have achieved average arithmetic returns in the 12% per year range, bonds in the 6% range, and cash equivalents in the 4% range. We concluded that these historical returns should represent reasonable expectations of what can be achieved in the future, over the long term. Obviously, short term returns can and undoubtedly will vary significantly from these long term expectations.

NOT ESTABLISHING OBJECTIVES: The 12% equities, 6% bond, and 4% cash returns should also function as our objectives for these investment categories. Later on in Chapter VI we set guidelines for asset allocation and combined long term returns with these asset allocation guidelines to arrive at investment objectives under all asset allocation scenarios.

NOT UNDERSTANDING RISK: Chapter III was devoted exclusively to discussing investment risk. We identified five different investment risks.

Market risk is the probability that a market will suffer a permanent or very lengthy decline in value. We concluded that equity, bond, and most cash equivalent markets do not carry with them the risk of permanent decline and therefore are the appropriate markets for most individual investors.

Credit risk was defined as exposure to a loss on a particular security, even if the market it is in does not decline. We concluded that credit risk can be avoided by broad investment diversification, and that market index mutual funds are an excellent way to achieve this diversification.

Liquidity risk is the inability to convert an investment to cash. We concluded that this risk can be avoided by avoiding (or at least limiting) investments in real estate, and using only reputable securities exchanges and financial institutions for all other investments.

Currency risk is exposure caused by your investment being denominated in a foreign currency. The obvious way to avoid this risk is to invest only in United States markets, or to at least limit the extent of investing internationally.

Volatility risk is the exposure to fluctuations in investment markets. This is the one risk that cannot be avoided. Therefore, each person's investment risk evaluation should result in an asset allocation which avoids the probability of having to sell investments at market bottoms. Funds needed for living or possible emergencies should be kept in safe, short term, very liquid investments.

NOT DETERMINING INVESTABLE ASSETS: Chapter IV was devoted exclusively to this issue. It stressed the importance of knowing your financial situation and, most important, the need to factor in all of your investment assets before you make a decision on investing any portion of these assets.

ACCEPTING POOR ADVICE: It would appear that the world is full of experts in economics, politics, and investing. We tried to point out that friends, relatives, and associates are generally not well equipped to dispense investment advice any more than they are equipped to give professional medical advice.

We cautioned against taking advice from those who sell investment products for a commission, namely brokers and financial planners. Their advice should be avoided unless they can demonstrate independently verified successful investment management performance.

We warned not to rely on the media to make your investment timing decisions. The media tends to report at market extremes and can be probably be considered, at best, a negative investment indicator. That is, when the headlines read how horrible a stock or real estate market is, it's probably indicative of a good time to buy.

TRYING TO TIME MARKET MOVES: Effective market timing is as close to an impossible game to win as any there is.

Pacific Financial Asset Management Corporation clearly pointed this out in a study of 1960-1990 investment performance which tracked the value of $1 invested in 1960 in the S&P 500 stock index. If the dollar was left alone for the entire period, it would have been worth $19.45 in 1990. If the investment was removed from the market in the 10 best performance months, it would have been worth only $6.58 in 1990, about the same as a 1960- 90 investment in treasury bills.

Market timing is not practiced successfully by most investment professionals and certainly is not a game that individuals can expect to win.

NOT DIVERSIFYING: Many of us in the investment business would point to diversification as the most important element in investing. Chapter III discussed it's importance in avoiding credit risk.

The fear that most people have of losing their money is usually due to not understanding the difference between market risk and credit risk. If investing is limited to markets that will continue to perform well as long as the underlying economies on which they are based continue to prosper, the only fear should be that your security selection will not do well. This is credit risk. It can be avoided with investments which represent the broad market, such as a group of actively managed mutual funds or, better still, index funds which are designed to track an entire market.

NOT COST AVERAGING: There is a difference between cost averaging and market timing. Market timing is a process of being in and out of a market, depending on your expectations for that market. Cost averaging is understanding and accepting that you don't know what a market is going to do in the short term and phasing a major purchase or sale to avoid transacting just before a major market move.

We pointed out how a major stock market investment just before the October 1987 market crash would have resulted in an immediate significant loss. If this investment had been phased over a several month period, much of that loss could have been avoided resulting in the investor having a significantly lower cost basis.

NOT MONITORING RESULTS: No matter how well you think your investments are doing or how passive your investment vehicles may be, you need to periodically look at them and to periodically re-evaluate your own personal financial situation.

Is the bank who's CD you hold in good financial shape? If not, is your money fully guaranteed? If not you should quickly move your funds elsewhere.

Are your active stock and bond funds performing to their benchmark levels? Has any underperformance been over an extended time period? Managers are not likely to highlight below-benchmark performance so the only way you can be sure is to keep track for yourself.

Even index funds need to be monitored. Is the fund approximating the market it is designed to track, or is it continually underperforming by more than investment fees and expenses?

Has your personal financial situation remained changed such that you have a different risk profile? Has your investment performance resulted in a significant shift in your asset allocation mix? Both can result in the need to revise your investment structure.

"HAVING NO "SELL" DISCIPLINE: "No" answers to the type of questions raised above mean that it's time to seriously consider one or more changes.

One of the most difficult things for all of us is to sell an investment. If the decision is because of underperformance, we are admitting defeat. If the decision is because of good performance and we are simply rebalancing, we hate to reduce an investment that has good to us. "Buying" is easy and "selling" is difficult. But you can't let emotions interfere with the prudent decision. If it's time to make a change, make it.

Chapter IX contained discussion of the specific rules that might be applied to monitoring your personal as well as manager performance.

CONCLUSION

This book has been devoted to providing individuals with a process for achieving investment results as good as the professionals who are successfully managing the billions of dollars of endowment and retirement funds comprising United States securities markets. There is no reason you cannot do as well as the best of them. You have access to the same information and most of the same investment vehicles as the pro's.

Changing your investment strategies and structure will take some time and patience, but not unreasonable amounts of either. Don't ignore your financial health any more than you would ignore your physical health.

Good investment wishes to all of you.

Subject Index